THE RAF
IN CAMERA

ALSO BY ROY CONYERS NESBIT

THE RAF
IN CAMERA

ARCHIVE PHOTOGRAPHS FROM THE PUBLIC RECORD OFFICE
AND THE MINISTRY OF DEFENCE

1946–1995

ROY CONYERS NESBIT

Assisted by Oliver Hoare

SUTTON PUBLISHING
IN ASSOCIATION WITH THE PUBLIC RECORD OFFICE

First published in the United Kingdom in 1996 by
Sutton Publishing Limited · Phoenix Mill · Thrupp · Stroud · Gloucestershire
in association with the Public Record Office

Reprinted 1997

British Library Cataloguing in Publication Data

A catalogue record for this book is available from the British Library.

ISBN 0-7509-1056-9 (hardback)

ISBN 0-7509-1522-6 (paperback)

 ALAN SUTTON™ and SUTTON™ are the trade
marks of Sutton Publishing Limited

Typeset in 11/15pt Baskerville.
Typesetting and origination by
Sutton Publishing Limited.
Printed in Great Britain by
WBC Limited, Bridgend.

CONTENTS

The historic church of St Clement Danes in the Strand, dating from the ninth century but rebuilt in its present form in 1681 by Sir Christopher Wren, was reduced to a shell by a bombing raid on 10 May 1941. Rebuilt once more, it was reconsecrated on 19 October 1958 as a centre of RAF worship in the presence of the Queen, Prince Philip, and other members of the Royal Family, as shown in this photograph. The electrically-operated bells rang out 'Oranges and Lemons' in celebration. Nowadays, Books of Remembrance in window recesses record the names of more than 125,000 men and women who died during the two world wars while serving in the RAF, the WRAF and associated women's services, the Commonwealth Air Forces, the RFC and the RNAS.

PRO ref: AIR 2/14501

INTRODUCTION

For many years, numerous photographs relating to the activities of the RAF have remained unrecorded in hundreds of documents in the Public Record Office (PRO) at Kew. Another large collection is housed in the Ministry of Defence in London. This series of three volumes is intended to bring representative photographs of both collections to the notice of the general public. The volumes are not intended to provide a comprehensive history of the RAF and its predecessors, but aim to give some indication of the huge numbers of photographs which are available.

In all cases the reference numbers of the photographs appear underneath the captions. The photographs at the PRO are not housed separately but the originals of each may be seen within their relevant documents by visitors who obtain readers' tickets and then request the numbers on computer terminals in the Reference Room. However, it should be noted that documents at the PRO are not normally available for public scrutiny until they are thirty years old, and the same stipulation applies to photographs. For this reason, the majority of the photographs in this third volume originate from the Ministry of Defence.

A catalogue of the many photographs kept at the PRO is available in the Reference Room, but at the time of writing this is by no means complete. A description of the contents of this catalogue is contained in PRO Records Information leaflet 90. Copies of RAF photographs, or any others found by readers, may be purchased via the Reprographic Ordering Section. Details such as choice of process and scale of charges are set out in PRO General Information leaflet 19. Copies of photographs are available for commercial reproduction from the PRO Image Library, telephone 0181-392-5255. Prices will be given on request.

The photographic prints relating to the RAF housed at the Ministry of Defence are not available for public inspection. The main purpose of this collection is to provide information to the RAF and various Government departments, and not to the general public. However, readers may write to the central library where negatives are held if they wish to purchase copies of photographs contained in these volumes or enquire about others. This is

CS(Photography)P, Ministry of Defence, Court 9 Basement, King Charles Street, London SW1A 2AH, with whom any purchasing arrangements may be made. At present this enormous collection covers the period from the very early days of the RAF and its predecessors up to the Gulf War of 1991. Some photographs in this book from the period after the Gulf War were obtained from RAF Publicity of the Ministry of Defence.

All the photographs in these three volumes are Crown Copyright. Guidelines for those who propose to reproduce photographs are set out in PRO General Information leaflet 15, and the same guidelines also apply to any photographs purchased from the Ministry of Defence.

This volume is the last of the series of three and covers the period after the Second World War up to the end of 1995. The photographs represent the Berlin Airlift, the Mau Mau rebellion in Kenya, anti-terrorist operations in Malaya, the Korean War, the atom bomb tests in Australia, the hydrogen bomb tests in the Pacific, operations in Cyprus, the Suez crisis, the Indonesian confrontation, the Falklands War and the Gulf War. Most post-war aircraft are included in the selection, as are some of the RAF's other activities such as air-sea rescue.

The captions underneath the photographs originate from the documents in which they were located in the PRO or the brief details available in the Ministry of Defence. This information was supplemented by a considerable amount of research in other documents in the PRO or reliable books of reference. Readers who wish to carry out similar research for the period up to 1965 are recommended to purchase a copy of PRO Readers' Guide No.8, *RAF Records in the PRO* by Simon Fowler, Peter Elliott, Roy Conyers Nesbit and Christina Goulter (PRO Publications 1994), available from the PRO Shop, Public Record Office, Ruskin Avenue, Kew, Richmond, Surrey TW9 4DU. This guide also includes an appendix which lists other sources of RAF photographs within Great Britain.

ACKNOWLEDGEMENTS

I should like to express my gratitude to Simon Fowler and Oliver Hoare of the PRO for their painstaking help in hunting for suitable photographs. Similarly, I am most grateful to Group Captain Ian Madelin RAF (Ret'd) and Squadron Leader Peter Singleton RAF (Ret'd) of the Air Historical Branch (RAF), the Ministry of Defence, for permission to include many official photographs housed in the MoD, as well as to Bill Hunt of the Whitehall Library for reproducing the MoD prints and Brian Carter for reproducing the PRO prints. My thanks are also due to Sergeant Rick Brewell of RAF Publicity who kindly provided some of his superb aerial photographs for the final section of the book and helped with their captions. I am extremely grateful to Squadron Leader Dudley Cowderoy RAFVR, Warrant Officer Jack Eggleston RAF (Ret'd) and Roger Hayward for their work in checking and correcting the captions. Any errors which remain after all this expertise are my own responsibility.

COLD WAR:
THE BERLIN AIRLIFT

After surface communication between the West and Berlin ceased with the imposition of a Russian blockade from 24 June 1948, the RAF and the USAF began a massive airlift to the city. Within a week the whole of RAF Transport Command's fleet of Avro Yorks and Douglas Dakotas had moved to Wunstorf, about twenty miles north-west of Hanover. The morning shift began at 02.00 hours. In this photograph, Sergeant John Parham is indicating to Aircraftman David Swain the dispersal point where a York needed servicing.

MoD ref: R1087

(*Opposite, top*) The aircrew of a York at Wunstorf planning their sortie to Gatow, the airfield in the British sector of Berlin used by the RAF. The USAF carried supplies to the airfield in the American sector, Tempelhof.

PRO ref: AIR 10/5067

(*Opposite, bottom*) The Flying Control at Wunstorf had to cope with a far greater flow of traffic than ever before. In this photograph, Aircraftman Charles Curran is using an Aldis lamp to flash a green light to the first Dakota in a wave of aircraft, giving the pilot permission to taxi along the perimeter track.

MoD ref: R1774

Enormous floats of supplies were stored in the hangars of airfields operating on the Berlin airlift. It was estimated that 4,500 short tons of food, coal and other essentials would have to be flown into the city each day by the RAF and USAF to supply the two-and-a-half million Berliners.

MoD ref: R1795

The aircraft were normally loaded from trains running into the airfields, but emergency dumps in the hangars were used if these failed to keep pace with demand. The Berlin airlift necessitated an immense and complex organization, with ground staff frequently working a sixteen-hour day.

MoD ref: R1796

The RAF staff in the control tower at Gatow were the first in the world to handle 800 aircraft movements a day. No mistakes were permitted and the work was extremely hard. In this photograph a controller is looking through a hatch into the R/T Monitoring Office to enquire about an aircraft which had called up.

MoD ref: R1833

A WAAF rigger, Corporal Kitty Wood, replacing the stabilizing fin and fitting a fairing on to an Avro York at Gatow on 16 September 1948, assisted by Aircraftman Fred Hames.

MoD ref: R1841

A special load of spares being loaded into York serial MW232.

PRO ref: AIR 55/118

A line of Avro Yorks of the RAF's Transport Command lined up at Gatow airfield in Berlin during the airlift, with serial MW287 of 242 Squadron in the foreground. The aircraft were marshalled in front of the hangars, where a German labour force unloaded them; unloading time averaged out at about ten minutes.

MoD ref: R1818

The Sunderlands of two flying boat squadrons and one operational conversion unit joined in the Berlin Airlift from July 1948, operating between Hamburg and Havel Lake, about five minutes by road from Berlin. These ground crews were photographed on 16 September 1948, sitting in the sun by the boathouse on Havel Lake while waiting for the next Sunderland to call up and give them its expected time of arrival.

MoD ref: R1832

A Sunderland V, serial VB389, of 201 Squadron after landing on Havel Lake on 16 September 1948, with its contents being loaded on to barges. The tonnage carried by the flying boats was quite small but the Berliners were impressed with their contribution. The Sunderlands continued to

operate until December 1948, by which time the lift by land-based aircraft into Berlin's airfields had increased considerably.

MoD ref: R1831

Lübeck in the British zone of Germany was one of three new despatching bases prepared for RAF aircraft. Pierced steel planking was laid down by German workers for the runway. Work continued at a very rapid pace and RAF Dakotas began to use the airfield in August 1948.

PRO ref: AIR 55/118

Civilian aircraft were also chartered to help in the airlift, such as this Dakota of Kearnley Airways being refuelled at Lübeck.

PRO ref: AIR 55/118

The Royal Army Service Corps handled much of the loading at Lübeck. From 27 August 1948 to 22 April 1949, 50,000 short tons were despatched from the airfield.

PRO ref: AIR 55/118

The airfield of Celle in the British zone of West Germany was made available to some of the Douglas C-54 Skymasters of the USAF, partly to help relieve congestion in the American bases of Rhein/Main and Weisbaden, and partly because Celle was nearer Berlin. The Skymaster carried about 10 tons and was a newer aircraft than the York, which could carry up to 9 tons. The rail sidings in this photograph, taken in November 1948, had been extended to bring up stone for forming the sub-base of the runway.

PRO ref: AIR 10/5067

RAF and USAF flyers looking at the target board on 16 September 1948 to check the progress of the airlift.

MoD ref: R1852

Facilities at Schleswigland airfield in the British zone of West Germany were improved to handle the new Handley Page Hastings of the RAF's 47 and 297 Squadrons, which began to replace Avro Yorks in September 1948. Two main loading areas were built, one to handle liquid fuel and the other for dry goods, while the runway was overlaid with asphalt. The Hastings began to operate from this airfield in November 1948, mainly carrying coal for Berlin's industries.

PRO ref: AIR 10/5067

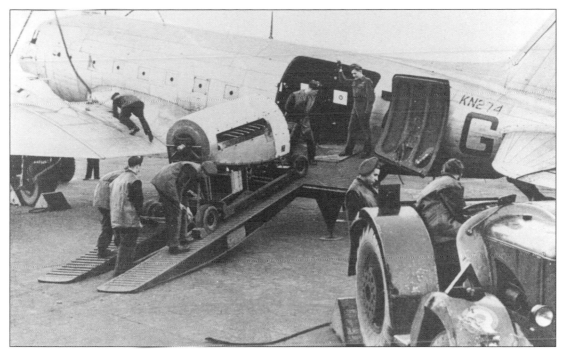

When RAF aircraft engaged on the Berlin airlift, such as this Dakota, serial KN274, they were sent back to the UK for periodic inspection and loaded with parts which needed repair. They returned with spares which were urgently needed.

PRO ref: AIR 10/5067

The RAF flew many children and elderly people out of Berlin to West Germany during the airlift, to reduce pressure on supplies when starvation was a possibility during the winter of 1948–9. The Russians lifted their blockade on 12 May 1949, but the RAF and the USAF continued to fly in supplies for several more months, to build up a stockpile in case of another emergency.

PRO ref: AIR 55/118

The Boeing B-29 Superfortress was known as the Washington by the RAF's Bomber Command when it was acquired at the beginning of the Cold War. Cocooned aircraft were taken out of storage and modernized, the first entering RAF service in August 1950. This photograph of Washingtons from 115 Squadron, based at Marham in Norfolk, was taken on 27 February 1951 during a training flight to Heligoland. The RAF began returning the machines to the USA in 1953 but a few continued in service until 1958.

MoD ref: PRB 1660

INTO THE JET AGE

The Gloster Meteor F8, such as serial WH320 in this photograph, was one of the series which began with the Meteor I supplied to 616 Squadron in July 1944. It entered squadron service in December 1949 and became the major type of single-seat day interceptor employed by the RAF for the next five years. It equipped twenty fighter squadrons as well as ten of the RAuxAF.

PRO ref: DSIR 23/22638

The de Havilland Vampire, which entered squadron service in April 1946, was the second jet fighter in the RAF. The Vampire FB5 was a fighter-bomber variant which followed in 1949. It became the most common type of jet fighter-bomber employed by the RAF until the de Havilland Venom began to appear in 1952. Subsequently, Vampires continued to serve overseas and in Flying Training Command. This photograph of Vampire FB5s of 603 Squadron, based at Turnhouse near Edinburgh, was taken shortly before the RAuxAF squadron disbanded in March 1957.

PRO ref: AIR 27/2712

The North American Sabre equipped RAF squadrons from May 1953 as a stopgap until the arrival of British swept-wing jets. It was a single-seat fighter capable of a maximum speed of 670 mph, primarily employed on defensive duties in West Germany. The machines were replaced by Hawker Hunters from the spring of 1955. These Sabres of 234 Squadron, serials XB885 and XB867, were photographed while in a vertical dive before entering cloud. The squadron was based in West Germany as part of the RAF's 2nd Tactical Air Force.

MoD ref: PRB9232

De Havilland Venoms of 23 Squadron landing at RAF Coltishall in Norfolk in 1955. This squadron was equipped with NF2s and NF3s, the two-seat night fighter version of the single-seat fighter-bomber.

PRO ref: AIR 28/1344

The English Electric Canberra was the first of Britain's jet bombers, entering RAF squadron service in May 1951. It succeeded the Avro Lincoln but was a light bomber with a crew of three. It was unarmed but fast and could carry a bomb load of 6,000 lb. The Canberra B6, with more powerful engines, was introduced in June 1954. This example of a B6, serial WH958 of 12 Squadron based at Binbrook in Lincolnshire, was photographed in September 1958. Some Canberra bombers were phased out when the V-Force of nuclear bombers was built up from 1955, but the reconnaissance versions continued in service.

MoD ref: PRB15899

Another version of the graceful English Electric Canberra was the B(1)8, such as serial XM245 photographed in September 1958 at the Farnborough Air Show. This was a night intruder, armed with four 20 mm guns in a pack beneath the fuselage and capable of carrying up to 5,000 lb of bombs. Four squadrons in Germany were equipped with Canberra B(1)8s from January 1958, and the machine continued in service until June 1971.

MoD ref: PRB15652

While based at Wunstorf in Germany during June 1956, 79 Squadron received Supermarine Swift FR5s to replace its Meteor FR9s. The earlier interceptor version of the Swift, the first swept-wing jet fighter to enter service in the RAF, had proved accident-prone when it was introduced into Fighter Command in February 1954, but it was hoped that a fighter/photo-reconnaissance version would be more successful in tactical work. Nevertheless, there was a high accident rate during the five years that the Swift FR5 remained in service with RAF Germany.

PRO ref: AIR 27/2794

Only twelve Supermarine Swift F7s were built, entering service in April 1957 with No. 1 Guided
Weapons Development Squadron at RAF Valley in Anglesey. It was powered by a Rolls-Royce
Avon 716 engine and fitted with Fireflash air-to-air missiles.

MoD ref: PRB15794

The Fairey Fireflash air-to-air missile was introduced into the Guided Weapons Development
Squadron at RAF Valley in 1957 but did not see service with operational squadrons. It was guided
to its target by a radar beam projected from the aircraft. This photograph showing Fireflash
missiles being wheeled to Swift F7s was taken on 16 October 1958.

MoD ref: PRB15838

The Hawker Hunter first entered squadron service in July 1954 as a single-seat day interceptor, becoming the RAF's standard fighter at home and in Germany until the arrival of the English Electric Lightning in June 1960. There were several variants of the machine, which could achieve Mach 0.95 at 36,000 feet. It possessed elegant lines and, with its responsive controls and excellent manoeuvrability, delighted pilots and spectators alike in aerobatic displays. This Hunter F6 was photographed while carrying rockets at the Farnborough Air Show in September 1958.

MoD ref: PRB15656

Hunter F6s of 63 Squadron lined up with the pilots and ground crews at Waterbeach in Cambridgeshire on 17 April 1957.

PRO ref: AIR 27/2791

HM The Queen and HRH Prince Philip visiting the Leuchars Wing, consisting of Venom and Hunter aircraft, at Fife on 4 June 1957.

PRO ref: AIR 28/1390

This Fairey Delta 2, serial WG774, powered by a Rolls-Royce Avon RA28 gas-turbine engine, was designed to achieve a world speed record of over 1,000 mph. It made its initial flight from Boscombe Down in Wiltshire on 6 October 1956, flown by Lieutenant-Commander L.P. Twiss. A second machine, serial WG777, flew for the first time on 15 February 1956. The attempt at the speed record was made on 10 March 1956 in serial WG774, flown by Twiss at 38,000 ft between Ford and Chichester in Sussex. He made two runs averaging 1,132 mph and became the first pilot in the world to exceed 1,000 mph. This photograph was taken in September 1958 at the Farnborough Air Show.

MoD ref: PRB15644

This Gloster Javelin FAW6, serial XA836, of 89 Squadron, photographed at Stradishall in Suffolk on 30 September 1957, was the first of this variant received by the squadron. The Javelin FAW1 entered service in February 1956 as the first twin-jet fighter in the world capable of high performance in all weathers.

PRO ref: AIR 28/1424

Vickers Valiant B1, serial XD816, converted to the tanker role, of 214 Squadron based at Marham in Norfolk, refuelling Gloster Javelin FAW7, serial XH887. This photograph accompanied the Air Estimates file of 1960–61.

PRO ref: AIR 19/1004

The English Electric Lightning F1 was the first of the RAF's supersonic fighters, entering squadron service in June 1960. F1s were followed five months later by these F1As (with a T4 trainer version in the foreground), fitted with refuelling probes, which were supplied to 56 Squadron at Wattisham in Suffolk. Powered by two Rolls-Royce Avon engines, the Lightning could achieve 1,500 mph at 36,000 feet, twice the speed of the Hawker Hunter it replaced. In addition to two 30 mm Aden guns, it carried two Firestreak air-to-air missiles.

MoD ref: PRB26377

This Lightning F1 of 74 Squadron was photographed at RAF Coltishall in Norfolk on 26 October 1963. The letters beneath the cockpit show that the machine was flown by Flight Lieutenant J.E. Brown while the ground mechanic was Chief Technician Rye.

MoD ref: PRB26227

This photograph of Hawker Hunter F6s, the variant of the famous single-seat interceptor which first entered RAF service in July 1954, appeared in an illustrated programme which accompanied a display held on 20 September 1958 at RAF Norton near Sheffield. This was the headquarters of No. 90 (Signals) Group.

PRO ref: AIR 28/1405

In June 1962 this Hunter T7, serial WV383, was photographed over Kai Tak in Hong Kong, at a time when 20 Squadron was converting from Venom FB4s to Hunter FGA9s. The T7 was the two-seat trainer version of the single-seat Hunter F4. The squadron remained equipped with Hunter FGA9s at Kai Tak until disbanding in January 1967.

MoD ref: CFP1056

Javelin FAW9, serial XH886, of 23 Squadron, based at Leuchars in Fife, photographed on 13 May 1963 while carrying a Firestreak air-to-air missile. The FAW9, the last of the Javelins, was fitted with an in-flight refuelling probe. The Firestreak missile, introduced into squadron service in 1958, was guided to its target by an infrared seeker cell in its nose.

MoD ref: PRB25293

Three Javelin FAW9s, serials XH887, XH708 and XH871, from 64 Squadron at Binbrook in Lincolnshire, fitted with their refuelling probes. They were photographed in October 1963 before the squadron flew out to Calcutta on an exercise. The squadron later provided defence for Singapore. It was disbanded in June 1967.

MoD ref: PRB26130

A Javelin carrying Firestreak air-to-air missiles, photographed with its crew in April 1963 at RAF Geilenkirchen in Germany. It was probably an FAW9 (without its refuelling probe) of 11 Squadron, which was based there at the time.

MoD ref: PRB25359

HOT WAR: KOREA, CYPRUS AND SUEZ

When the Korean War broke out in June 1950, the RAF at home had been drastically reduced after the Second World War, while the Far East Air Force was fully stretched dealing with the Malayan Emergency. Nevertheless, Britain was committed to help the USA resist the communist invasion, as a member of the United Nations. Apart from advice and guidance, with some officers serving with the US 5th Tactical Air Force, the RAF contributed Sunderlands of the Far East Flying Boat Wing. Detachments of 88, 205 and 209 Squadrons flew to Iwakuni on the southern tip of Honshu, Japan, where they came under American command. This photograph was taken on 14 November 1950.

MoD ref: CFP876

The Sunderland Vs of the three RAF squadrons carried out over 1,100 lengthy sorties from their base in Japan, flying on anti-submarine and maritime patrols around North Korea. The results of their reconnaissance work enabled the Americans and British to blockade Korean ports and plan their carrier-borne strikes.

MoD ref: CFP297

Soldiers of the Middlesex Regiment after disembarking from the Hastings troop carrier. All British and Commonwealth brigades were formed into the 1st Commonwealth Division on 28 July 1951.

MoD ref: CFP258

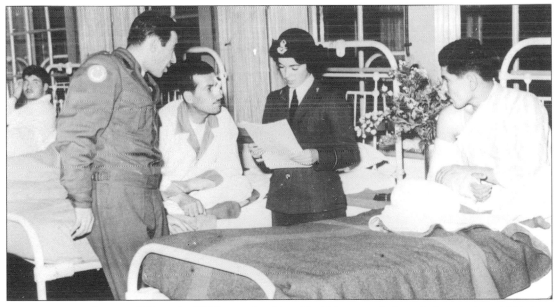

Nursing Sister Flying Officer G. Williams checking Turkish wounded on 5 September 1951 in a ward of Sick Quarters, No. 91 Wing RAAF, Iwakuni. This was to ensure that the men were fit to fly under her medical charge to Singapore.

MoD ref: CFP438

British brigades were formed to participate in the Korean War, mainly from Commonwealth regiments. Some of these soldiers were flown from Japan to Pusan in Korea by Handley Page Hastings of 48 Squadron, normally based at Changi in Singapore. The Hastings troop carrier in this photograph was being guided into position by an American controlman on 10 October 1950.

MoD ref: CFP257

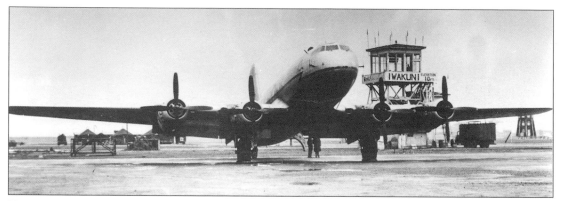

Hastings, serial TG520, of 48 Squadron taxiing out on 5 September 1951 before take-off from Iwakuni airfield for a two-day flight to Singapore, via Clark Field in Manila, with twenty-eight wounded. This was the eighth flight since the squadron began casualty evacuation from Japan during the previous February.

MoD ref: CFP433

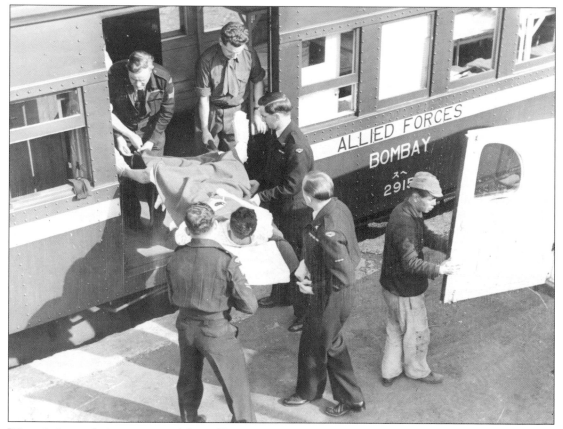

Wounded men being evacuated from Korea on 15 July 1953, twelve days before the armistice was signed at Panmunjon. By this time, approximately 350,000 men of the United Nations had been killed or wounded, while enemy casualties were estimated as not less than 1,500,000.

MoD ref: CFP752

Guerrilla operations began in Cyprus on 1 April 1955, when EOKA (Ethniks Organosis Kypriou Agonistou) exploded a series of bombs in an attempt to ensure that the island was ruled by Greece, against the wishes of the Turkish minority. The first RAF counter-guerrilla operations took the form of searching the sea approaches, to prevent the landing of illegal weapons, and reconnaissance over land by light aircraft and helicopters. On 15 October 1956, 284 Squadron was re-formed in Nicosia with Sycamore HAR14s for general purpose activities and casualty evacuation. This photograph is of a stream take-off with a contingent of the King's Own Yorkshire Light Infantry.

MoD ref: CMP876

A soldier of the King's Own Yorkshire Light Infantry absciling down a rope from a Sycamore helicopter of 284 Squadron. The method of landing small bodies of troops gave the security forces the advantage of surprise over EOKA bands in the Troodos mountains. Operations continued until Cyprus became an independent republic on 21 September 1960, with Britain retaining sovereignty over certain military bases.

MoD ref: CMP877

When diplomacy failed after Egypt nationalized the Universal Suez Canal Company on 26 July 1956 in defiance of the treaty of 1888, the British and French decided to recover their rights by force. One of the main airfields available for a preliminary air attack on the Egyptian Air Force was RAF Nicosia in Cyprus. On 31 October 1956, Wing Commander Peter Dobson was photographed in the briefing tent while giving crews of the Bomber Wing their instructions for an attack on Kabrit airfield, north of the town of Suez. Thirty-one MiG-15s had been identified here from photo-reconnaissance carried out by Canberra PR 7s of the RAF and Republic F-84s of the French Air Force.

PRO ref: AIR 28/1474

A weapons briefing given on 31 October 1956 to the Bomber Wing by Flight Lieutenant G. Webster in the briefings tent at Nicosia, preparatory to an attack against Almaza airfield, near Cairo, where photo-reconnaissance had revealed twenty-four MiG-15s.

PRO ref: AIR 28/1474

This photograph was taken on 24 July 1956 at Upwood in Huntingdonshire when 61 Squadron took part in the Air Officer Commanding's parade and inspection. The squadron was equipped with Canberra B2s and on 22 and 23 October of that year, flew out to Nicosia as part of the Suez operation, which was code-named 'Musketeer'.

PRO ref: AIR 27/2756

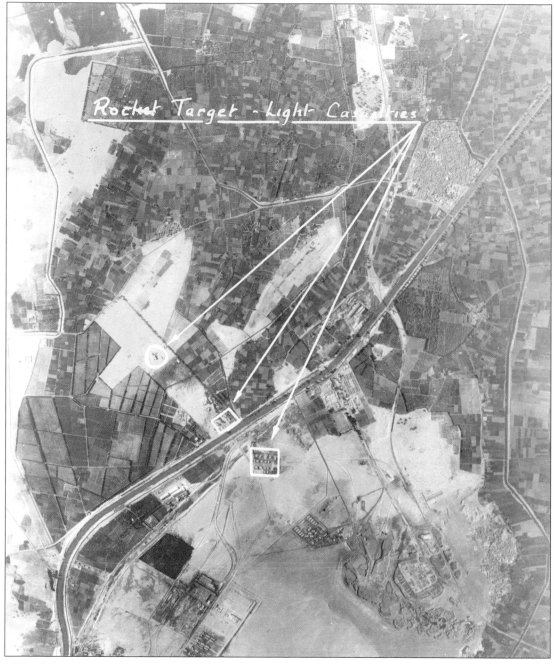

Rocket Target - Light Casualties

This photograph of radio transmission stations at Abu Zabac in Cairo was taken on 18 March 1955 by a Meteor PR 10 of 13 Squadron based at Abu Sueir, at a time when there was still an RAF presence in Egypt. It was used as a target map by the RAF during the Suez crisis. The main radio station was bombed on 2 November 1956 by twenty Canberras of the Cyprus Wing, escorted by twelve Republic F-84s of the French Air Force. It went off the air but soon came back on a different frequency.

PRO ref: AIR 20/10215

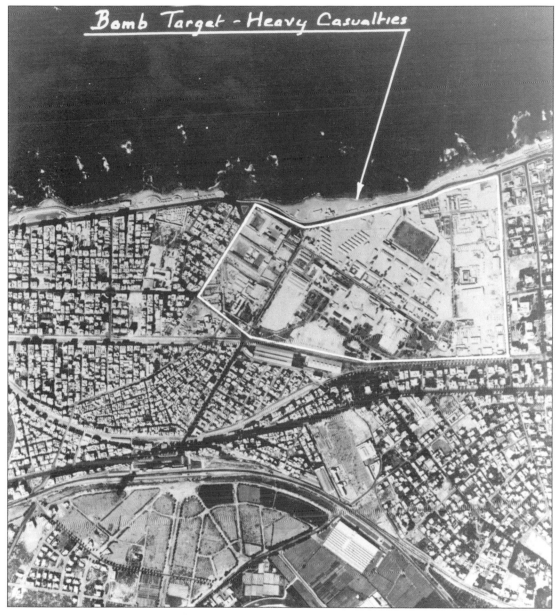

This photograph of Mustapha Barracks in Alexandria was also used as a target map by the RAF. It was taken from 30,000 feet on 13 October 1955 by a Meteor PR 10 of 13 Squadron based at Abu Sueir.

PRO ref: AIR 20/10215

Another target map used during the Suez operation was this photograph of oil installations in Cairo, taken on 19 January 1956 by a Meteor PR 10 of 13 Squadron based at Abu Sueir. The last RAF units left Egypt on 17 May 1956.

PRO ref: AIR 20/10215

The RAF's Bomber Wing at Nicosia consisted of six squadrons of Canberra B2s, comprising fifty aircraft, and one squadron of twelve Canberra B6s, all sent out from England. In this photograph taken from the Control Tower, the Canberras were taking off to attack Luxor airfield, further south beside the Nile, on the evening of 2 November 1956. Photo-reconnaissance had revealed twenty-two Ilyushin Il-28 light bombers on this airfield. A Canberra B2 of 27 Squadron is in the foreground, with Meteor NF13s of 39 Squadron and Hunter F4s of 1 Squadron on the right of the runway.

PRO ref: AIR 28/1474

There was so much congestion at Nicosia and Akrotiri in Cyprus that a second bomber force was established at Luqa in Malta for the attack on Egypt, although this island was further from the targets. This force included four squadrons of the new Vickers Valiant B1, the first of the four-jet strategic V-Class bombers which had entered RAF service in February 1955. Twenty-four Valiants had arrived at Luqa by 30 September 1956, although they did not carry the nuclear bombs for which they had been designed.

MoD ref: CMP829

In addition to the Valiants at Luqa, four squadrons of Canberra B2s and B6s arrived at Halfar in Malta from England, comprising twenty-nine aircraft. They joined in the high-level attacks against Egyptian airfields which began in the afternoon of 31 October 1956. This photograph was taken when armourers were bombing up Canberra B2, serial WH951, with 1,000 lb medium-capacity bombs.

MoD ref: CMP853

A Canberra taking off from Halfar for an attack on Egyptian airfields. The Allied aircraft taking part in the operation were painted with 'invasion stripes', consisting of two black and three yellow.

MoD ref. CMP841

A Valiant taking off from Luqa for an attack on Egyptian airfields.

MoD ref: CMP825

Valiant crews being debriefed at Luqa after a bombing raid on Egyptian airfields. After three days, it was estimated that 158 enemy aircraft had been destroyed from the total of 195 originally photographed on the airfields. No aircraft of the RAF or French Air Force were lost from enemy action in these attacks, although a Venom of 8 Squadron, which was among those making low-level attacks from Akrotiri, hit the ground and the pilot was killed.

MoD ref: CMP821

In the early hours of 5 November 1956 a force of eighteen Valettas and fourteen Hastings, led by a Hastings of 114 Squadron, took off from Nicosia for a dropping zone alongside Port Said's Gamil airfield, as shown in this photograph. Each aircraft carried about twenty men of 3 Battalion Parachute Regiment as well as heavy equipment. At the same time, the French Air Force carried French paratroops from Tymbou in Cyprus. Meanwhile, Venoms from Akrotiri strafed the defences of the airfield and Hunters from Nicosia provided top cover, supported by carrier-borne squadrons from the Royal Navy's task force. The paratroops captured the airfield after stiff fighting and all aircraft returned, although nine transports were hit by anti-aircraft fire. Further drops took place in the afternoon.

PRO ref: AIR 27/2758

In the early morning of 6 November 1956, Royal Marine commandos and units of the Royal Tank Regiment stormed the beaches of Port Said, as shown in this photograph of landing craft approaching the shore while covered by helicopters. At the same time, French paratroops and commandos landed nearby at Port Fuad. These assaults were preceded by a naval bombardment and supported by air attacks.

MoD ref: X65958

Fierce fighting with casualties took place at Port Said. There was also damage to property during street clearance, as shown in this photograph taken after the conflict. The British forces were able to link up with the French and start moving down the Suez Canal, but the Security Council of the United Nations insisted on a cease-fire, which took place on the day of the seaborne assaults. Although a military success, the Anglo-French intervention in Egypt was a political failure.

PRO ref: WO 32/16686

THE NUCLEAR AGE

By 1951 Britain had decided to catch up with the United States and Russia with the explosion of an atomic bomb. The site chosen for the first experiment was a lagoon off Hermite Island, in the uninhabited Monte Bello Islands off the coast of Western Australia, as shown in this photograph.

PRO ref: AIR 8/2308

(*Opposite*) This dramatic photograph was taken on 8 November 1957 when Britain exploded her fourth H-bomb. It was dropped from Valiant XD825 flown by Squadron Leader Barney T. Millett, off South East Point, Christmas Island. Each of these H-bombs contained the equivalent of a million tons of TNT and created a mushroom shape up to 60,000 feet high, with ice caps forming on top.

MoD ref: PRB14263

A Lancaster tailplane, placed at 6,707 feet, broadside to the blast, photographed before the explosion.

PRO ref: AIR 8/2309

The elevator was torn off by the force of the blast.

PRO ref: AIR 8/2309

(*Opposite, top left*) The first British atomic bomb was exploded on 3 October 1952 in the frigate HMS *Plym* moored in the lagoon off Hermite Island. The top photograph was taken thirty seconds later, while the bottom one was taken one minute after the explosion, showing a water column and cloud.

PRO ref: AIR 8/2309

(*Opposite, top right*) Two-and-a-half minutes after the explosion.

PRO ref: AIR 8/2309

(*Opposite, bottom*) Seven-and-a-half minutes after the explosion.

PRO ref: AIR 8/2309

After the first explosion in the Monte Bello Islands, alternative sites were sought on land. The next explosions took place on 14 and 16 October 1953 from towers erected on the Emu Field of South Australia. The camp site in this photograph was close to the centre line of the Long Range Weapons Establishment at Woomera.

PRO ref: AVIA 65/1118

The Monte Bello Islands were chosen again for the next nuclear explosions. The RAF collaborated, with photo-reconnaissance Canberras of 542 Squadron sent from Weston Zoyland in Somerset to RAAF Laverton in Western Australia to provide high-level monitoring of radiation and other results. The first experiment took place on Trimouville Island on 16 May 1956 and the second on Alpha Island on 19 June 1956. Observers had to turn their backs for several seconds. Although the bombs were considered small, eerie orange flashes could be seen from hundreds of miles away.

PRO ref: AIR 20/10812

A whole series of A-bomb tests followed in the remote area of Maralinga, or 'Loud Thunder' in the Aborigine language, north of the Nullarbor Plain in South Australia. Explosions took place on 27 September, 1956; 4, 11 and 21 October 1956; 14 and 25 September 1957, and 9 October 1957. Five of these seven tests took place from towers or at ground level. Of the others, the explosion of 11 October 1956 is especially noteworthy since it was the first nuclear bomb dropped by the RAF, from a Vickers Valiant B1 detached from 49 Squadron at Wittering in Northamptonshire and flown by Squadron Leader E.J.G. 'Ted' Flavell. The test of 9 October 1957 took place from an assembly of barrage balloons and the bomb exploded at 300 feet. Meanwhile, the RAF was beginning a series of tests with hydrogen bombs in the Pacific.

PRO ref: AVIA 65/1118

A Centurion Mark II tank after the explosion of an A-bomb at Maralinga.

PRO ref: WO 320/1

A Daimler Scout Car Mark II and dummy soldier, subjected to the blast of an A-bomb at Maralinga.

PRO ref: WO 320/1

In 1956 Vickers Valiant B1s of 49 Squadron at Wittering were being prepared to carry Britain's new hydrogen bomb, which weighed 10,000 lb. The crews trained with the object of testing the H-bomb at Christmas Island, a British possession in the central Pacific slightly north of the Equator. This photograph was taken at Wittering before three aircraft set off to fly westwards across North America and Hawaii to the remote island.

MoD ref: PRB13079

Wing Commander Ken G. Hubbard (on ladder) about to enter Valiant serial XD818 at Wittering, followed by his crew, before taking off on the flight to Christmas Island. On 15 May 1957 he and his crew dropped Britain's first H-bomb near the southern tip of Malden Island, south-east of Christmas Island. It was released from 45,000 feet and set to explode at 8,000 feet. Three more H-bombs were dropped on Malden Island, on 31 May, 19 June and 8 November 1957. Then five more bombs were exploded off Christmas Island, in 1958. These were dropped from a Valiant on 28 April, from a balloon assembly on 22 August, from Valiants on 2 and 11 September, and from a balloon assembly on 22 September.

MoD ref: PRB13075

The men on Christmas Island took part in sports and amused themselves with competitions such as the greasy pole. This photograph was taken on 29 December 1958, over two months after the last British hydrogen bomb was exploded from a balloon assembly.

PRO ref: AIR 28/1700

The Duke of Edinburgh visited Christmas Island on 3–5 April 1959, after the end of the British hydrogen bomb tests. He was photographed while inspecting a detachment of Hastings C1 transports of 36 Squadron, with serial TG557 in the foreground. 217 Squadron was also based at Christmas Island from 14 February 1958 to 13 November 1959, equipped with Whirlwind HAR 2s. The squadron was then disbanded.

PRO ref: AIR 28/1700

The Duke of Edinburgh on his tour of inspection of Christmas Island on 3–5 April 1959. The United States carried out a further series of tests on the same sites during the following year. In 1979, Christmas Island became part of the Republic of Kiribati, an independent member of the British Commonwealth. The islands of Malden and Jarvis, where the explosions took place, remain uninhabited.

PRO ref: AIR 28/1700

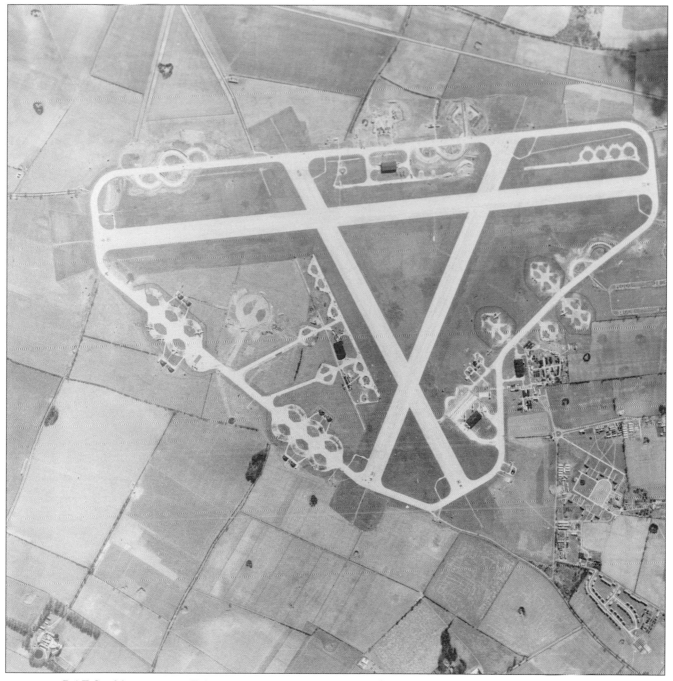

RAF Sculthorpe, near Fakenham in Norfolk, was opened as a bomber station in 1943. It became one of the main bases for reconnaissance aircraft of the USAF's Strategic Air Command during the Cold War. For several years, from 1951, aircraft flew from this station on spy flights over Russia to photograph Soviet nuclear bases. This photograph, taken on 15 March 1951, shows the three runways, one of 3,000 yards length and two of 2,000.

PRO ref: AIR 14/3702

The Avro Vulcan B1 was the second of Britain's V-Class bombers, entering RAF service in July 1956 as part of the nuclear strike force. This Vulcan B1, serial XH497, of 617 Squadron at Scampton in Lincolnshire was photographed on 10 November 1958. In June 1961 a Vulcan of this

famous 'dam-buster' squadron flew non-stop from Scampton to Sydney in Australia, refuelled in the air by Valiant tankers. The flight of 11,000 miles was achieved in 20 hours 3 minutes.

MoD ref: PRB15986

A Blue Steel, the strategic air-to-surface missile with a thermonuclear warhead, developed by Hawker Siddeley Dynamics, being loaded in Vulcan B1, serial XA903, for early trials. The photograph accompanied the Air Estimates papers of 1960–61. The Blue Steel missile finally became operational in February 1963.

PRO ref: AIR 19/1004

This Handley Page Victor B1, serial XA923, of No. 232 Operational Conversion Unit at Gaydon in Warwickshire, flown by Flight Lieutenant A.J.A. Heyns, was photographed in April 1958 while landing at Wyton in Cambridgeshire to join the RAF's Radar Reconnaissance Flight. The Victor was the last of the RAF's three V-bombers, entering service in November 1957 and continuing in this role until 1968. Some were converted to tankers and continued working for many more years.

PRO ref: AIR 29/2999

The Bristol-Ferranti Bloodhound 1 was a surface-to-air missile with a nuclear warhead. From 1958, it was deployed in units of sixteen by Fighter Command in defence of RAF V-bomber bases. This Bloodhound 1 was photographed on 19 November 1958 at RAF North Coates in Lincolnshire, while HRH The Duke of Edinburgh watched it traversing and following a target aircraft.

MoD ref: PRB16001

Vickers Valiant B1, serial XD859, of 214 Squadron based at Marham in Norfolk, converted to the tanker role, refuelling Avro Vulcan serial XA910 of 101 Squadron based at Finningley in Yorkshire. This photograph, taken on 4 November 1959, accompanied the Air Estimates file of 1960–61.

PRO ref: AIR 19/1004

An Avro Vulcan flying over RAF Gan, a remote staging post built on Addu Atoll in the Maldive Islands. The station became operational in August 1957 and was used mainly by RAF aircraft flying over the Indian Ocean to and from Singapore. This photograph accompanied the Air Estimates documents of 1960–61.

PRO ref: AIR 19/1004

One of the visitors to the Far East Air Force was this Victor B1, serial XA926, of 10 Squadron from Cottesmore in Rutland. The machine was taking part in a mobility exercise when photographed on 27 November 1960 while flying at low-level over the coast of Malaya and providing an impressive spectacle to the local people.

MoD ref: CFP1006

THE FAR EAST BUSH WARS

Avro Lincoln *Excalibur*, serial RF484, of a Special Flight at Blackbushe in Hampshire, photographed before departure at 05.00 hours on 9 September 1946 for New Zealand. Lincolns arrived too late to succeed Lancasters in the Second World War but twenty squadrons of Bomber

Command were equipped with these machines. They saw service during the Mau Mau uprising in Kenya and the Malayan Emergency. They were withdrawn in 1963.

PRO ref: AIR 29/476

After the vicious Mau Mau rebellion broke out in Kenya in 1952, the RAF allocated aircraft to support the police and the security forces. Vampire FR9s from 8 Squadron based at Khormaksar in Aden were detached in late 1953 to Eastleigh near Nairobi to help in attacks against terrorist

gangs. These Vampire FR9s were photographed at 16,000 feet while returning from an anti-bandit strike with rockets. Mount Kenya is in the background.

MoD ref: PRB8146

Avro Lincoln B2s of 49 Squadron arrived at Eastleigh in November 1953 from Wittering in Northamptonshire. They were succeeded in January 1954 by Lincolns of 100 Squadron and then by Lincolns of 61 Squadron, all from the same base. Aided by photographic reconnaissance and intelligence reports, the Lincolns carried out a bombing campaign against terrorists hiding in the Aberdare mountains. The Lincoln could carry up to 14,000 lb of bombs and the dismayed terrorists began to come out of the bush to surrender. By early 1955 most of the Mau Mau gangs had been broken up. The RAF's participation in the state of emergency ended in December 1956.

MoD ref: PRB8154

This Westland Dragonfly HC 2, serial WF311, was photographed in February 1950 while being used for trials. The machine was of American design but built in Britain. It carried a pilot with provision for three additional passengers or two stretchers. The first Dragonflies were sent to Malaya and formed the Far East Casualty Evacuation Flight at Seletar in Singapore on 1 April 1950, which became 194 Squadron at Sembawang in Singapore on 1 February 1953. Dragonflies carried out some remarkable work in the Malayan Emergency but they were tiring to fly and serviceability was low in jungle conditions.

PRO ref: PRO 58/54

When emergency powers were invoked in June 1948 against Communist terrorists in the newly-created Federation of Malaya, ageing but reliable C-47 Dakotas were available for service from the RAF. One of their duties was supply dropping to ground forces, employing the successful techniques developed in the Burma campaign of the Second World War. This photograph was taken on 2 July 1951.

MoD ref: CFP427

A training unit was set up in Singapore during June 1950, equipped with Tiger Moths and Harvards, as one of the four squadrons forming the re-created Malayan Auxiliary Air Force. The squadrons, with locally recruited pilots and ground staff, served on short-range transport and visual reconnaissance duties, including anti-terrorist operations, until entering the Royal Malayan Air Force which was established in 1958.

PRO ref: INF 10/316

(*Opposite, top*) In August 1948 three Beaufighter TFXs of 45 Squadron were detached from Negombo in Ceylon to Kuala Lumpur in the fight against Communist terrorists. They proved so successful with their striking power of four 20 mm cannons in the nose and eight rockets under the wings that Beaufighters of 84 Squadron were sent up from Singapore to join them. The remainder of 45 Squadron arrived at Kuala Lumpur on 16 May 1949, when it began to convert to Bristol Brigands. This photograph of a Beaufighter of 45 Squadron being serviced was taken on 10 August 1948.

MoD ref: CFP90

(*Opposite, bottom*) In April 1951 de Havilland Hornet F3s entered service with 33 Squadron at Butterworth near Penang in Malaya, replacing ageing Hawker Tempest F2s. This photograph, taken on 23 April 1952, shows aircraft both parked and taxiing on the airfield.

MoD ref: CFP538

These five Vampire FB5s were photographed on 2 December 1950 at the RAF Maintenance Base at Seletar in Singapore after six had arrived from the UK. Their flight of 8,500 miles was completed in 27¾ flying hours. With its excellent performance and fire power, strong construction and ease of maintenance, the Vampire proved ideal for conditions in Malaya. No. 60 Squadron at Kuala Lumpur received Vampire FB5s in December 1950, replacing Spitfire PR9s, and the squadron continued to operate with these machines until Vampire FB9s arrived two years later.

MoD ref: CFP353

A formation of de Havilland Vampire FB9s of 60 Squadron, based at Tengah in Singapore, photographed on 26 August 1952 when *en route* to bomb Communist camps in the Malayan jungle.

MoD ref: CFP620

The de Havilland Hornet was a long-range fighter with two Rolls-Royce Merlin engines, which first entered RAF squadron service in May 1946. These Hornet F3s of 45 Squadron, based at Tengah, were photographed on 26 August 1952 while en route to attack Communist positions in south Malaya, armed with cannons and rockets.

MoD ref: CFP606

Avro Lincolns of 1 (RAAF) Squadron arrived at Tengah on 16 July 1950 and remained on the station for almost eight years, operating against Communist terrorists. This photograph was taken on 26 August 1952.

MoD ref: CFP642

This series of photographs was taken on
26 April 1950 and constructed as a mosaic.
It shows bombs being dropped by Avro
Lincolns of 57 Squadron from Tengah, with
others exploding on Communist camps in
the Segamat district of Johore.

MoD ref: CFP285

500 lb bombs being dropped on Communist positions by a Lincoln of 1 (RAAF) Squadron on 26 August 1952. The maximum bomb load of the Lincoln was 14,000 lb.

MoD ref: CFP644

Lincolns of 1 (RAAF) Squadron taxiing back to their dispersal points at Tengah after attacking Communist positions on 26 August 1952.

MoD ref: CFP640

Recruitment to the new RAF Regiment (Malaya) from local volunteers began on 1 April 1948 when 91 Rifle Squadron was formed at Kuala Lumpur. Four other Rifle Squadrons were formed later, their original duties being the protection of RAF bases. In June 1948, 91 Squadron also began duties alongside the Army in anti-terrorist work. This photograph was taken in Selangor on 18 August 1952 when A Flight was moving through an oil palm grove in search of a wounded bandit.

MoD ref: CFP582

Airmen of A Flight, 91 Rifle Squadron, RAF Regiment (Malaya) on stand-to with a scout car at a post in Selangor, photographed on 15 August 1952. They were facing an area of rubber trees outside an estate manager's house which had been requisitioned and occupied by the Flight.

MoD ref: CFP577

Airmen of the RAF Regiment (Malaya) preparing to fire a mortar. This photograph was taken on 26 August 1952.

MoD ref: CFP619

The Scottish Aviation Pioneer first entered RAF service in February 1954 with 267 Squadron at Kuala Lumpur. With remarkably short take off and landing runs, it was used for internal security work and for supplying jungle forts. This example was serial XJ465 of 267 Squadron.

MoD ref: CFP978

Spitfire PR 19, serial PS836, of 81 Squadron based at Seletar in Singapore, photographed on 10 March 1954 while on a photo-reconnaissance sortie over a coastal region of Malaya. The last operational flight of any Spitfire was made on 1 April 1954 by 81 Squadron's Spitfire PR 19, serial PS888.

MoD ref: CFP845

Airmen of the RAF Regiment (Malaya), led by Warrant Officer J.J.H. Nichols, circling through a mangrove swamp on 17 July 1954, on the hunt for any boats carrying food to terrorists.

MoD ref: CFP850

The Bristol Sycamore was the first helicopter designed in Britain to enter RAF service, the prototype making its first flight on 24 July 1947. In October 1954, Sycamores began to supplement the Westland Dragonfly HC 2s of 194 Squadron for search and rescue missions in Malaya. The machine carried a crew of two, with three passengers or two stretcher cases and the cruising speed was about 20 mph faster than the Dragonfly. This Sycamore HAR 14, serial XF266, of 194 Squadron was photographed while alighting in a jungle clearing to pick up a casualty.

MoD ref: CFP937

Ground staff of 33 Squadron photographed at Butterworth on 23 March 1955 while loading up a Hornet F3, serial PX328, with two 500 lb bombs. The aircraft had already been armed with four rockets fitted with 60 lb high explosive warheads under the wings and four 20 mm cannons in the nose. It was one of three preparing to make the 5,000th sortie against Communist terrorists in Malaya.

MoD ref: CFP856

Squadron Leader N.P.W. Hancock, the Officer Commanding 33 Squadron, taxiing out to lead the three Hornet F3s on their operation. The squadron lost its identity eight days later when it was merged with 45 Squadron on the same station.

MoD ref: CFP854

This photograph was taken in November 1955 during a radar-siting expedition into the Malayan jungle, headed by Squadron Leader H.E. Bennett. The equipment was a portable radio station employing HF/DF or Morse code. From June 1956 research resulted in the mobile 'Target Director Post' which provided a narrow beam, down which aircraft flew towards the target until receiving a signal telling them to release the bombs. This equipment was the AA GL Radar No. 3 Mk 7, and an average error of 175 yards was achieved at a range of 40,000 yards. Of course, its effectiveness depended on the accurate location of terrorist positions, which was often achieved by aerial photo-reconnaissance.

MoD ref: CFP907

The Hunting Percival Pembroke was a communications aircraft, with a crew of two and accommodation for eight passengers, which entered service with RAF squadrons in September 1954. It was also used for training pilots, navigators and signallers. In January 1956, six of these machines were converted into Pembroke PR 1s and supplied to 81 Squadron at Seletar in Singapore, where they joined in the process of surveying Malaya, an operation which had begun with the squadron's Mosquito PR 34s in July 1949 and was continuing with Meteor PR 10s. From these surveys, updated maps on scales of one inch to a mile and a quarter inch to a mile were continually provided for the ground forces. This photograph is of serial WV746 of 152 Squadron, which began to receive Pembrokes in October 1958, while based at Muharraq in Bahrain. Pembrokes continued in RAF service until 1988.

MoD ref: PRB1260/22

This de Havilland Mosquito PR 34A, serial RG314, of 81 Squadron, based at Seletar in Singapore, was the last operational Mosquito in service with the RAF. The photograph was taken on 5 January 1956 but the aircraft made its final sortie on 16 December 1956, photographing Communist positions in the Malayan jungle. By that time, 81 Squadron had converted to Gloster Meteor PR 10s.

MoD ref: CFP921

Venom FB4s of 8 Squadron being refuelled at Kormaksar in Aden in 1957. In August of that year, a detachment formed part of a small RAF force sent to Sharjah and Bahrain in the Persian Gulf to assist the Sultan of Muscat and Oman in suppressing a Communist insurrection in the interior. Operations continued with the SAS and other regiments until successfully concluded in February 1959.

MoD ref: CMP911

(*Opposite, top*) Men of the RAF Regiment (Malaya) going into action from a Westland Whirlwind HAR 4 helicopter of 155 Squadron, photographed on 13 April 1957 when the squadron was based at Kuala Lumpur. With a crew of three, the machine could achieve rapid deployment of up to five fully-armed troops but it suffered from poor serviceability in jungle conditions, exacerbated by the difficulty of obtaining sufficient spare parts.

MoD ref: CFP966

(*Opposite, bottom*) This photograph was taken when Bristol Sycamore HAR 14, serial XJ918, of 14 Squadron, based at Changi in Singapore, paid one of its regular visits to a landing pad made from bamboo and leaves alongside a jungle fort in north Malaya. The men standing are, left to right: Chief Technician Wilfred Lloyd, Flight Lieutenant Albert Cann (pilot), Dr Malcolm Bolton (employed by the Malayan Government) and a medical orderly. Those seated were members of the Sakai aborigines living in the locality. The time was near the end of the Malayan Emergency, and regulations were finally lifted on 31 July 1960.

MoD ref: CFP1162

Sunderland V, serial DP198, of 205 Squadron, based at Seletar, flying over the waterfront at Singapore. This was the last RAF operational squadron equipped with Sunderlands, which were fully withdrawn by May 1959. Serial DP198 was 'struck off charge' on 1 June 1959.

MoD ref: CFP985

This Bristol Type 192 helicopter, serial XG451, was photographed in November 1959 during tests with various take-off weights. The helicopter division of Bristol was absorbed by Westland during the following March. The machine entered RAF service in December 1961 as the Westland Belvedere, fitted with two twin-rotor engines of 1,600 shaft horse power. Employed on carrying freight and troops, casualty evacuation and supply dropping, it saw operational service in Tanganyika, South Arabia and Borneo before being retired in March 1969.

PRO ref: AIR 2/15354

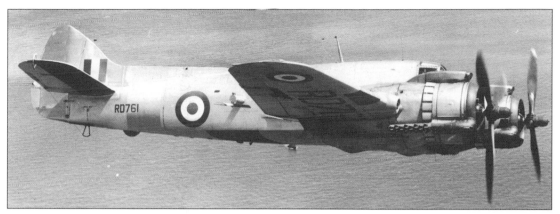

On 12 May 1960 the last Beaufighter in RAF service, serial RD761 employed as a target-tower, made its final flight from RAF Seletar in Singapore.

MoD ref: CFP1003

In December 1960 a detachment of Beverleys of 47 Squadron was sent from Abingdon in Berkshire to Eastleigh in Kenya, to reinforce British Forces Arabian Peninsula (BFAB) which had a base there and to help with famine relief after severe flooding and crop failure. There was also a threat of violence while negotiations for independence were in progress. This photograph was taken in March 1961 at Nanyuki in Kenya, showing troops of the King's African Rifles disembarking from Beverley serial XB286. Kenya achieved independence on 12 December 1963, although the British presence continued for another year to help suppress dissension in the north of the country.

PRO ref: AIR 27/2866

On 21 August 1962 Sycamore HR14, serial XE310, of 110 Squadron, based at Butterworth in Malaya, dropped a member of the SAS Regiment into the jungle near the Thai border, where a few Communist terrorists were still in hiding in the hope that they could foster another insurrection. The purpose was to rescue an injured pilot of a crashed Auster aircraft of the Army Air Corps. Meanwhile, a party from the SAS Regiment worked its way through the thick jungle.

MoD ref: CFP1052

At the end of 1962, a confrontation with the Indonesian Republic developed, following the objection of the latter to the proposition that the British Crown Colonies of Sarawak and Sabah and the British Protectorate of Brunei, be incorporated with Malaya and Singapore into a new Federation of Malaysia. Insurrections were fomented in Brunei and to help deal with these, troops were airlifted from Singapore to RAF Labuan, an island off the coast of Sabah. Among these were men of the 1st Battalion, The Queen's Own Cameron Highlanders, who were flown out from Seletar on the night 9/10 December 1962 in Beverleys of 34 Squadron. They were photographed while unloading stores at RAF Labuan.

MoD ref: CFP1065

On 10 December 1962, British and Gurkha troops were flown out of RAF Labuan to airstrips near the towns of Seria and Anduki, which were under siege by the rebels. Five Scottish Aviation Twin Pioneers took off for Seria, while one Beverley of 34 Squadron left for Anduki. The soldiers quickly subdued the insurgents at both places but armed rebellion continued elsewhere in North Borneo.

MoD ref: CFP1064

The Twin Pioneers of 209 Squadron continued to take men into and out of small jungle-enclosed airstrips, as shown in this photograph of British troops emplaning on serial XL970 from an airstrip in the Fifth Division of Sarawak, after the formation of the Federation of Malaysia on 16 September 1963. Twin Pioneers were also used for carrying equipment, supply-dropping to small jungle outposts and broadcasting messages by voice to the civil population.

MoD ref: CFP1148

The single-engined Pioneers of 209 Squadron, with their landing runs of 66 yards and take-off runs of 75 yards, proved invaluable for getting in and out of the very small airstrips in Borneo. This light communications aircraft could carry a pilot and four passengers, and was sometimes used for casualty evacuation.

MoD ref: CFP1174

British troops moving into action from Twin Pioneers of 209 Squadron.

MoD ref: CFP1066

Hunter FGA9, serial XJ683, of 20 Squadron, carrying twelve 3-inch rockets, photographed while flying past the twin peaks (known as the Ass's Ears) on the jungle-covered island of Pulau Tioman off the east coast of the Malayan Peninsula. The Hunter FGA9 was converted from the home-based F6 for tropical work. The machines began to fly out to Tengah in Singapore during July 1961, where 20 Squadron was re-formed the following September. This became one of the principal defence squadrons of the Far East Air Force. The squadron was also engaged on patrols from RAF Labuan and RAF Kuching during the confrontation with Indonesia.

MoD ref: CFP1182

Handley Page Hastings also brought troops from RAF Changi in Singapore to RAF Labuan at the beginning of the confrontation with Indonesia. These transports were also engaged on dropping supplies to ground forces, as shown in this photograph of a Hastings fitted with long-range tanks flying over Belaga in Sarawak.

MoD ref: CFP1078

Sycamore HAR14 after touching down at Bongau in Sarawak, having come through a narrow gap between the trees in the background. These light helicopters were ideal for work in the small clearings of the North Borneo jungles.

MoD ref: CFP1156

A Whirlwind HAR10 taking off from a dusty forward airstrip in the far east of Sarawak. This mark of helicopter, which was fitted with a turbine engine instead of the piston engine of the Whirlwind HAR4, first entered RAF service in November 1961. Two squadrons based at Seletar were equipped with these machines, which could carry a crew of three and eight passengers. These were 110 Squadron from July 1963 and 103 Squadron from August 1963, both of which served in North Borneo. They were joined there by 225 Squadron in December 1963 and 230 Squadron in March 1965, both arriving from the UK.

MoD ref: CFP1161

A Whirlwind HAR10 helicopter of 225 Squadron picking up a Gurkha patrol to ferry them to a jungle outpost in Sarawak. This photograph was taken in 1964.

PRO ref: CFP1187

The first RAF squadron to be equipped with the new Westland Belvedere helicopter was 66 Squadron at Odiham in Hampshire. In May 1962 the squadron moved to Seletar, where this photograph was taken. The twin-rotor Belvedere could carry eighteen fully-armed troops in addition to its crew of two; twelve stretcher cases, or a load weighing up to 6,000 lb.

MoD ref: CFP1048

A Belvedere of 66 Squadron lifting an Army truck from RAF Kuching in Sarawak. It was bound for a forward outpost where troops were guarding a potential entry point against infiltration by Indonesian soldiers.

MoD ref: CFP1150

The Hawker Siddeley Argosy C1 was a medium-range tactical transport, capable of carrying a crew of four and about seventy troops, which entered RAF squadron service in February 1962. In August 1963, 215 Squadron arrived at Seletar with these machines and began operating over North Borneo, primarily on transport and supply-dropping duties. This photograph was taken in January 1964 during an exercise in Malaya, when troops and equipment were being loaded into an Argosy at RAF Changi in Singapore.

MoD ref: CFP1081

This photograph, taken in January 1964 from an Argosy of 215 Squadron, illustrates the almost impenetrable terrain of North Borneo, with winding rivers and jungle-clad mountains. The frontier with Indonesia was 800 miles long but fortunately there were only a few feasible points of entry for incursions from Indonesia, which were guarded by British and Commonwealth troops. The whole area was surveyed by Canberra PR 7s of 81 Squadron from Singapore, assisted by Canberra PR 7s of 13 Squadron detached from Malta. Maps were made from the resulting photographs and used by the ground forces.

MoD ref: CFP1080

Anti-aircraft Bofors guns of 40 mm calibre on the airfields at Singapore were manned by the RAF Regiment, in case the Indonesian Air Force decided to mount air attacks during the confrontation. A number of 20 mm Bofors guns were also transferred from naval reserve to boost the air defences.

MoD ref: CFP1191

These men of 15 (Field) Squadron of the RAF regiment were among those detached from Singapore to guard airfields in North Borneo. In fact, the Indonesian Air Force was reluctant to make incursions into the territory, which was patrolled by Hunter FGA9s and Javelin F9s of the RAF.

MoD ref: CFP1173

An airfield in North Borneo guarded by an aircraftman of the RAF Regiment. There was little problem with internal security after the initial riots had been put down, for the great majority of the population supported the security forces. Incursions into North Borneo became so costly for the intruders that they began to peter out. A peace treaty was signed between Malaysia and Indonesia on 11 August 1966.

MoD ref: CFP1175

THE LEARNING CURVE

The Vickers Valetta first entered RAF squadron service in May 1949 as a medium-range transport capable of carrying thirty-four troops or freight, in addition to its crew of four. It continued in this capacity until April 1966 but meanwhile, in 1950, the Valetta T3 entered service as a navigation trainer. This photograph of Valetta T3, serial WG259, showing six astrodomes used by trainee navigators, was taken on 22 March 1954.

MoD ref: PRB7578

The trainee navigators busy at work inside Valetta T3, serial WG259.

MoD ref: PRB7574

The Bristol Brigand was designed to replace the Beaufighter TFX as Coastal Command's torpedo bomber, but, when torpedoes were replaced by rockets, its role was switched to that of ground attack carrying up to 2,000 lb of bombs. It first entered service at RAF Habbaniya in 1949 and subsequently saw service against terrorists in Malaya, employing guns, bombs and rockets. From July 1951 some Brigands were converted to trainers for radar night-fighting duties such as this T5, serial VS837, of the Air Interception Course at RAF Colerne in Wiltshire, photographed on 3 March 1955. These trainers were finally withdrawn from RAF service in March 1958.

MoD ref: PRB9411

The Vickers Varsity T1 was an advanced crew trainer for pilots, navigators and bomb aimers which first entered RAF service in October 1951 and continued until finally withdrawn in May 1976. This prototype, serial VX828, made its maiden flight on 17 July 1949.

MoD ref: PRB817

The Percival Prentice began to replace the long-serving Tiger Moth in November 1947 as the RAF's *ab initio* two-seat trainer. It continued as a trainer for pilots until 1953, although within this period the Chipmunk was introduced as a replacement. It was also employed for training signallers and carrying out communications duties.

MoD ref: PRB3008

The de Havilland Chipmunk became the main replacement for the Tiger Moth and the Prentice as the RAF's basic trainer after its introduction in February 1950. It was gradually withdrawn from 1973 after the introduction of the Scottish Aviation Bulldog, although some continued in service until the late 1980s. These Chipmunks of No. 18 Reserve Flying Training School at Fairoaks in Surrey were photographed in 1951.

MoD ref: PRB2301

The Boulton Paul Balliol T2 was a two-seat advanced trainer with a piston engine, which first entered the RAF's Flying Training Schools in 1952. It continued in service for about four years, when it was superseded by jet aircraft. This example, serial VW899, photographed 6 September 1950, was one of four prototypes.

MoD ref: PRB814

The Handley Page Marathon was originally built as a short-haul airliner but in December 1953 an adapted version was supplied to the RAF as a navigation trainer. This version, known as the Marathon T11, carried a pilot, wireless operator, an instructor and two trainee navigators. It was fitted with astrodomes and teardrop windows. This Marathon T11, serial XA274, served with No. 1 Air Navigation School at RAF Topcliffe in Yorkshire. Twenty-eight of these machines were supplied, finally being withdrawn in June 1958.

MoD ref: PRB6923

The Hunting Percival Jet Provost T1 was introduced as an experiment during 1955 for primary jet training. Only ten were delivered, to 2 Flying Training School at Hullavington in Wiltshire. Instructors formed a Jet Provost Team named the *Red Pelicans*, painted red and white, for display purposes. This photograph was taken at the Central Flying School at Little Rissington in Gloucestershire in 1964, showing the team in delta formation.

MoD ref: PRB27275

Cadets of the Air Training Corps, photographed on 21 October 1958 during a week's gliding instruction course at RAF Hawkinge in Kent.

MoD ref: PRB15867

A statue of Lord Trenchard, first Marshal of the Royal Air Force and first Chief of the Air Staff, was unveiled on 19 July 1961 in the Victoria Embankment Gardens opposite the Air Ministry by the Prime Minister, the Rt. Hon. Harold Macmillan.

PRO ref: AIR 2/16130

The Hawker Siddeley Gnat was a two-seat jet trainer which entered service with No. 4 Flying Training School at RAF Valley in Anglesey during November 1962. The machine was designed for high performance flying and could exceed the speed of sound in a slight dive. This photograph was taken on 29 April 1963. Two years later, RAF Valley formed its own aerobatic team of Gnats, painted yellow and known as the *Yellowjacks*. This advanced trainer remained in RAF service until November 1978.

MoD ref: PRB24960

Aircraft apprentices at the School of Technical Training, RAF Halton in Buckinghamshire, photographed in March 1963 while removing a gun pack from a Hunter which had previously served with 74 Squadron.

MoD ref: PRB24919

A poster printed in April 1964 which may have struck terror into the hearts of many RAF recruits. It showed thirty-seven articles of an airman's kit laid out for inspection on his bed. However, the official RAF nomenclature had become somewhat less formal by that date. For instance, 'Brush, shoe, polishing' had become simply 'Shoe Brush'.

PRO ref: AIR 2/15168

The Hawker Siddeley Dominie T1 was the first jet aircraft specially designed as an advanced navigation trainer when it entered RAF service in December 1965. This machine, serial XS730, was in service with No. 1 Air Navigation School at RAF Stradishall in Suffolk when photographed in 1966. The machine carries two pilots, a navigation instructor and two trainee navigators, with accommodation for one other crew member. In 1995, Dominies remained in service with No. 6 Flying Training School at RAF Finningley in Yorkshire.

MoD ref: PRB33187

The Scottish Aviation Bulldog T1 is a piston-engined aircraft with the seats side-by-side, employed by the RAF and University Air Squadrons as a primary trainer. It first entered service in April 1973 and is still a standard trainer. The three nearest Bulldogs in this photograph, serials XX659, XX658 and XX657, are currently with Cambridge University Air Squadron at RAF Cambridge, while the furthest aircraft, serial XX644, is with Bristol University Air Squadron at RAF Colerne in Wiltshire.

MoD ref: TN7311/2

The Scottish Aviation Jetstream was introduced into the RAF from June 1973 as a multi-engined trainer for pilots in the transport fleet, but soon afterwards the machines were placed in storage as a result of defence cuts. Some were reintroduced during 1977. This Jetstream serial XX497, with two turbo-prop engines, is on the strength of No. 5 Flying Training School at RAF Finningley in Yorkshire.

MoD ref: TN7636/17

The Shorts Tucano, designed in Brazil, was selected in 1985 as the RAF's basic trainer and began to enter service three years later with Flying Training Schools. It has a single turbo-prop engine and the two seats for instructor and trainee pilot are arranged in tandem.

MoD ref: TN9990/3

MARITIME
RECONNAISSANCE AND
SEARCH & RESCUE

The Lockheed Neptune MR1 was supplied to the RAF's Coastal Command from January 1952 as a stopgap while Avro Shackletons were coming into service. A long-range maritime reconnaissance aircraft with a crew of seven, it could carry a bomb load of up to 8,000 lb. Four home-based squadrons were equipped with the Neptune, but the machines were returned to the USA from 1956. This photograph was taken on 9 June 1953 when Neptunes were returning from a patrol.

MoD ref: PRB6474

Avro Shackleton MR2, serial WL751, of 224 Squadron over Gibraltar, where the squadron was based from May 1953 to October 1966 while equipped with these machines. The Shackleton was developed from the Lincoln, the MR1 entering service in April 1951, with the MR2 following late in the following year. Known affectionately as '10,000 rivets flying in close formation', variants of the reliable Shackleton formed the mainstay of the RAF's maritime reconnaissance force until 1970. After this, an airborne early warning version continued until the early 1990s.

MoD ref: CMP898

On 1 March 1956 the 550-ton motor vessel *Greenhaven* developed engine trouble in heavy seas off Eire and was driven on to the Roaninish rock, two miles from the coast of Donegal. She began to break up and her crew of ten abandoned the vessel and huddled together in bitter cold on the highest reef of the rock. During the night, the anti-submarine frigate HMS *Wizard* from Londonderry directed her searchlights on the scene to help a lifeboat from Arranmore, but the heavy seas prevented a landing. An air-sea rescue Shackleton MR1A, serial WB828 letter C, flown by Pilot Officer K.H. Wilson, from 120 Squadron at Aldergrove in County Antrim, was called out to assist in the early hours of the next day. The aircraft dropped flares to guide the lifeboat but no rescue was possible. Blankets and food were dropped from the port window as soon as it was light. At 08.00 hours two naval helicopters arrived from Eglinton, near Londonderry, and lifted off the ten marooned men. They were landed at Portnoo, on the coast nearby, and survived their experience.

PRO ref: AIR 27/2761

On 23 May 1953, thirteen pilots from RAF Church Fenton in Yorkshire participated in a demonstration of air-sea rescue. Each in turn was lifted from a dinghy in Bridlington Bay by a Sycamore of 275 Squadron from RAF Thornaby and then landed on the Ground Control Interception station at Bempton, on the shore nearby. Smoke floats were dropped to indicate wind direction and strength to the helicopter pilots.

PRO ref: AIR 27/2718

Air-sea rescue launch 2758, from the RAF's Marine Craft Unit at Newhaven in Sussex, photographed while travelling at high speed on 24 September 1958.

MoD ref: PRB15766

On 31 December 1961 a distress message was received at RAF Changi in Singapore from the Italian vessel SS *Galatea*, which had run aground at night on Pearsons Reef in the South China Sea. A Shackleton MR1A of 205 Squadron, based at Changi, was sent out on a search-and-rescue mission. The vessel was located on the northern and weather side of the reef. Heavy seas were breaking over her, but she did not seem in any immediate danger of sinking.

PRO ref: AIR 27/2985

The destroyer HMS *Caprice* was diverted to the scene to effect a rescue. Three further sorties were flown by Shackletons of 205 Squadron in co-operation with the Royal Navy. On 2 January 1962, the weather moderated sufficiently for the destroyer to rescue all twenty-two Italian seamen on board SS *Galatea*.

PRO ref: AIR 27/2985

Flight Sergeant Eric C. Smith, a winchman in the crew of a Whirlwind HAR10 of 22 Squadron at RAF Chivenor in Devon, was awarded a George Medal for his part in the rescue of French fishermen from the 273 ton trawler *Jeanne Gougy* on 4 November 1962. The trawler from Dieppe had been driven onto rocks at Land's End during the previous night. She was swept by twenty foot breakers while people watched helplessly from the cliffs. Rocket lines fired from the shore proved unsuccessful. A lifeboat from Sennen in Cornwall picked up bodies from the sea but was unable to reach the trawler. One seaman was rescued by a wire lowered by a Whirlwind from Chivenor. At about 11.30 hours another Whirlwind, serial XJ428 flown by Flight Lieutenant J.T. Eggington, arrived. Four more survivors were picked up in turn by the wire lowered from the helicopter. The others were too weak to get into the strop so Flight Sergeant Smith was lowered and went into the wheelhouse. The trawler was lying on her side and the situation was extremely dangerous. Nevertheless, he came out with one semi-conscious man and was winched up. He then returned and came back out of the wheelhouse with the cabin boy, to the cheers of amazed onlookers. He made one more descent to look for other survivors but the danger became so acute that he was ordered to return to the helicopter.

MoD ref: PRB24731

On 13 August 1963 the winchman of a Westland Whirlwind HAR10 of 228 Squadron, based at Leconfield in Yorkshire but detached to Leuchars in Fife, was lowered to pick up the skipper of the Peterhead drifter *Sustain*, who was suffering from suspected appendicitis. The skipper was then flown to Aberdeen for hospital treatment.

MoD ref: PRB25948

The Westland Wessex HC2 first entered RAF squadron service in January 1964 as a short-range helicopter for tactical transport and ground assault, capable of carrying up to sixteen troops as well as its crew of three. It served in Germany, the Arabian Gulf, Cyprus, Hong Kong, Singapore and Malaysia as well as at home. From May 1976, it found an important niche as an RAF search-and-rescue helicopter around the coasts of Britain. This Wessex HC2, serial XR502, of the Wessex Intensive Trials Unit at RAF Odiham in Hampshire was photographed in 1963.

MoD ref: PRB25906

The Hawker Siddeley Nimrod was evolved from the Comet airliner to supply the RAF with a marine reconnaissance aircraft as a replacement for the long-serving Shackleton. The first Nimrod MR1s entered RAF service in October 1969. The MR2s, with more advanced electronic equipment, followed in 1975. This Nimrod MR2, serial XV228, of 206 Squadron from RAF Kinloss in Morayshire, was photographed in July 1981 by Sergeant Jerry Chance of RAF Public Relations while flying over an oil rig in the Moray Firth. The aircraft remained in service in 1995, with the Kinloss Marine Reconnaissance Wing.

MoD ref: 080/5G

Sergeant Mark Redmond of 42 Squadron at RAF St Mawgan in Cornwall, demonstrating the use of the Nikon FA camera from the open beam window of a Nimrod MR2 in 1992. This is the latest camera to be used by Nimrod squadrons. It contains a 35 mm film which takes 36 exposures and gives superb definition.

MoD ref: 491/92G

The RAF Mountain Rescue Service originated on an *ad hoc* basis in 1942 when airmen who survived crashes in mountainous areas within the UK were losing their lives from injuries and exposure. It developed into a formal organization during the following year. This photograph of a Mountain Rescue Training Course in the Ben Nevis area, with Aonach Berg in the background, was taken in February 1963. The teams work in coordination with RAF search-and-rescue helicopters, which frequently transport them to the area of a crash. They deal with the search and rescue of civilians as well as RAF personnel.

MoD ref: PRB24749

Sea King HAR3, serial XZ593, of 202 Squadron from RAF Leconfield in Yorkshire, photographed in July 1991 by Sergeant Rick Brewell of RAF Public Relations while flying over Flamborough Head.

MoD ref: 654/29

Nimrod MR2, serial XV235, of the Marine Reconnaissance Wing at Kinloss in Morayshire, photographed on 7 May 1992 by Sergeant Rick Brewell of RAF Public Relations while flying over the nuclear submarines HMS *Trenchant* and USS *Spadefish* when they broke through the ice at the North Pole. The ice was too thin on this occasion for the British and American crews to play their usual game of football at the annual rendezvous.

MoD ref: 689/7

SPANNING THE GLOBE

The military version of the Bristol Britannia civil airliner provided RAF Transport Command with a turbo-prop aircraft for strategic operations. This example, serial XL635, named *Bellatrix*, was the first handed over, to 99 Squadron at Lyneham in Wiltshire on 9 June 1959. All Britannias were given the names of stars. They remained in service until January 1976.

MoD ref: PRB16804

A military version of the de Havilland Comet airliner, the first turbo-jet to operate commercial services, entered the RAF's Transport Command in July 1956. Known as the Comet 2, it was employed on long-distance transport duties, with a crew of five and accommodation for forty-four passengers. A version with a longer fuselage and seats for ninety-four passengers entered service in February 1962. It was named the Comet 4, such as serial XR397 in this photograph. Comets remained in RAF service until June 1975.

MoD ref: PRB25033

The Beagle Basset CC1 was an adaptation of a civil executive aircraft, first entering RAF squadron service in 1965. It was intended for the transport of V-bomber crews but its range and performance proved insufficient for this purpose and it was transferred to other light communications until it was withdrawn in 1974. The Basset in this photograph, serial XS743, was one of two used for performance trials at RAF Boscombe Down in Wiltshire before twenty production aircraft were ordered for the RAF.

MoD ref: PRB29016

British Aircraft Company VC10s began to arrive with 10 Squadron at Fairford in Gloucestershire in July 1966. These machines improved the RAF's 'rapid reaction' capacity, each being able to transport 150 troops for over 3,500 miles without refuelling, or double the range with in-flight refuelling. Thirteen VC10s were supplied to 10 Squadron, all named after RAF personnel who had been awarded the Victoria Cross. This machine, serial XV102 named after Guy Gibson VC, was photographed while flying over the Scilly Isles. Other VC10s were converted from civil airliners to the tanker role. In 1995, 10 Squadron at Brize Norton in Oxfordshire still operated ten VC10s in the transport or dual tanker role while 101 Squadron at the same station was equipped with nine machines in the tanker role.

MoD ref: PRB37465

The Short Belfast, a near-relative of the Britannia airliner, was introduced into RAF squadron service in January 1966 as a long-range military transport with turbo-prop engines. It was the first British aircraft designed solely for that purpose, and could carry up to 150 troops or 80,000 lb of freight. Only ten were built, allocated to 53 Squadron, which was disbanded in September 1976. They were all given names, such as serial XR366 *Atlas* in this photograph, which was taken on the Belfast Proving Flight at RAF Boscombe Down in Wiltshire.

MoD ref: PRB31844

The turbo-prop Lockheed Hercules C1 became the mainstay of the RAF's tactical transport fleet after its introduction into squadron service in August 1967. This Hercules serial XV177, the first to be camouflaged in RAF markings, was photographed in 1967 at RAF Boscombe Down in Wiltshire. In 1995 the machine was still in service with the RAF Lyneham Transport Wing but, as with several others of the Hercules fleet, it has been 'stretched' by lengthening the fuselage by fifteen feet. It is designated a Hercules C3 and can carry up to 128 troops, in addition to the crew of five.

MoD ref: T6985

Lockheed TriStar K1 tanker, serial ZD951, of 216 Squadron refuelling a Tornado in flight.

MoD ref: 0095/6

THE FALKLANDS
AND GULF WARS

When Argentine forces invaded the Falkland Islands on 2 April 1982, followed by the dependency of South Georgia the following day, Britain was drawn into a conflict on behalf of territories which had been under her protection for over 200 years. The resulting war was fought by combined forces, in which the RAF and the Fleet Air Arm played a prominent part. The American staging airfield of Wideawake on the British island of Ascension, situated in the Atlantic about halfway along the 8,000 miles between the Falklands and London, proved indispensable in these operations. Two Hercules, three Victors and one VC10 of the RAF can be seen in this photograph, as well as a C-141 Starlifter of the USAF.

MoD ref: H3287/1

A stream of supplies was carried to Wideawake airfield by Hercules of the RAF's Transport Wing based at Lyneham in Wiltshire. The aircraft were refuelled in flight by Victor K2 tankers from Marham in Norfolk.

MoD ref: H3286/1

A Hercules of the RAF's Lyncham Transport Wing, showing its refuelling probe, at Wideawake airfield.

MoD ref: H3281

The first elements of the South Atlantic Task Force sailed from Portsmouth on 5 April 1982 bound for Ascension Island and then the Falklands. They were led by the aircraft carriers HMS *Hermes* (photographed here) and HMS *Invincible*.

MoD ref: H3300/1

The liner SS *Canberra*, 43,975 grt, disgorged 1,600 passengers when she arrived at Southampton on 7 April 1982 at the end of a world cruise. She was rapidly fitted up for the South Atlantic Task Force and soon became capable of carrying up to 5,000 troops such as Royal Marines and Commandos. Two helicopter flight decks were lifted into position. This photograph was taken when the liner was moored at Ascension Island.

MoD ref: H3285/1

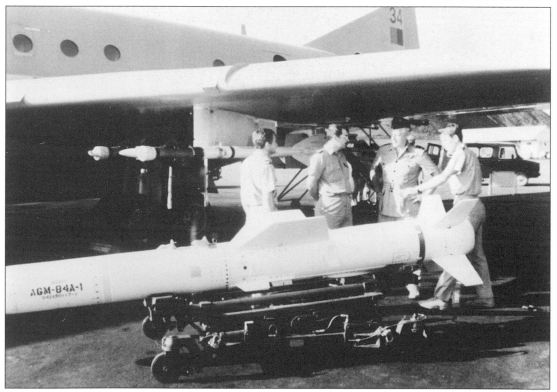

The Nimrod MR2s were then modified with refuelling probes so that from 9 May they were able to fly on maritime sorties of up to nineteen hours when refuelled by Victor K2 tankers. Their role was to hunt for Argentine vessels and submarines and then attack any which entered the 200-mile exclusion zone declared by the British around the Falklands. Meanwhile, some of the Victors were converted to the reconnaissance role and employed on very long-distance work. From 20 April, they reconnoitred South Georgia, which was re-taken five days later by a small task force of the Royal Navy from Gibraltar.

MoD ref: H3284/1

(*Opposite, bottom*) Nimrod MR1s of 42 Squadron from St Mawgan in Cornwall flew out to Wideawake. They were followed on 12 April by Nimrod MR2s of 120, 201 and 206 Squadrons from Kinloss in Morayshire, which were equipped with more effective Searchwater radar. The Nimrods were armed with McDonnell Douglas Harpoon anti-shipping missiles, as shown on the trolley in this photograph. This weapon is radar-guided and has a range of 75 miles at a speed of Mach 0.85. The aircraft were additionally fitted with pylons which enabled them to carry four Sidewinder air-to-air missiles, as can also be seen in this photograph.

MoD ref: H3303/3

Stanley Airport on the Falklands was attacked in the early hours of 1 May by a Vulcan B2 of 44 Squadron, with a crew from 101 Squadron. The aircraft flew from Wideawake, refuelled *en route* by a succession of Victor tankers, and dropped a stick of twenty-one 1,000 lb bombs across the runway. The purpose was primarily to deny the use of the airfield to the Mirages and Super Etendards of the Argentine Air Force from the mainland, which might have been able to operate from there with the aid of arrester gear. More attacks followed at dawn against the airport and a grass airfield at Goose Green by Sea Harriers of the Task Force, the aircraft carriers and other vessels having sailed from Ascension Island on 16 April.

MoD ref: H3288/1

Between 3 and 5 May, nine Harrier GR3s of the RAF's 1 Squadron flew from Wittering in Northamptonshire to Wideawake, refuelled en route by Victor tankers.

MoD ref: H3283/1

Six of the Harrier GR3s embarked on the container ship MV *Atlantic Conveyor*, which left Ascension for the Falklands on 8 May. Four Chinook HC1 helicopters from the RAF's 18 Squadron at Odiham in Hampshire were also carried on this vessel. All the aircraft were cocooned against the elements and lashed firmly to the deck. Three Harriers remained at Wideawake for defensive purposes, but they embarked later, together with five more, after being replaced by Phantom FGR2s of 29 Squadron from Coningsby in Lincolnshire.

MoD ref: H3292/1

On 18 May the six Harrier GR3s began flying from the container ship MV *Atlantic Conveyor* to the aircraft carrier HMS *Hermes*. Eight more flew to the carrier from Wideawake by means of in-flight refuelling. The role of these RAF Harriers was to relieve the FAA Sea Harriers from air-to-ground duties, enabling these to concentrate on combat with Argentine aircraft flying from the mainland on anti-shipping attacks.

MoD ref: H3205/1

The decks of HMS *Hermes*, 28,700 tons displacement, were covered with aircraft. This photograph shows an RAF Harrier GR3 armed with Paveway 1,000 lb laser-guided bombs, together with two more RAF GR3s, in front of FAA Sea Harriers fitted with fuel tanks and armed with 30 mm cannons and Sidewinder missiles, with an FAA Sea King in the background. The FAA Sea Harriers and helicopters of the two aircraft carriers formed the largest part of the air strike force, although some of the Sea Harriers were flown by RAF pilots on attachment to the Royal Navy. Light helicopters of the Royal Marines and the Army Air Corps also made an essential contribution.

MoD ref: H3280/1

The pilots of the Argentine Air Force attacked the vessels of the South Atlantic Task Force with great courage, flying Dassault-Breguet Mirages, Douglas A-4P Skyhawks, Israel Aircraft Industries Daggers and Dassault Super-Etendards from bases on their mainland. In spite of very heavy losses, some succeeded in firing Aérospatiale AM.39 Exocet sea-skimming missiles. The container ship MV *Atlantic Conveyor* was hit on 25 May, as shown in this photograph. She sank three days later. In the course of the campaign, the Argentines also sank two destroyers, two frigates, a Royal Fleet auxiliary, and badly damaged another auxiliary.

MoD ref: H3275

Three of 18 Squadron's Chinook helicopters were destroyed when the container ship MV *Atlantic Conveyor* was hit by the Exocet missile. On the night of 20/21 May, men of the British amphibious force began landing at San Carlos. On 9 June, an airstrip with 800 feet of aluminium planking was opened nearby in order to enable the Harrier GR3s (which were not able to align their inertial system sufficiently accurately to return to the aircraft carriers without assistance) to operate from the mainland. The remaining Chinook carried out prodigious work after the landings, ferrying troops and supplies from vessels to the mainland. It was disgorging fuel drums when this photograph was taken.

This solitary Chinook was photographed while transporting a truck inland. However, the greatest part of the work of ferrying and casualty evacuation was carried out by helicopters of the Fleet Air Arm, such as Sea Kings, Lynxes and Wessexes. Army and Royal Marine helicopters also played an important part in these operations.

MoD ref: H3290/1

On 28 May, British amphibious forces landed at Goose Green in East Falkland and captured the town after a stiff battle. This IA.58A Pucarà of III Brigada Aerea was photographed after the re-occupation. A turbo-prop aircraft of the Argentine Air Force, it was capable of operating from small airstrips as well as from Stanley Airport.

MoD ref: H3297/1

The RAF lost four Harrier GR3s, three by ground fire and one in an accident. This crashed GR3 was photographed while a British Commando was looking at a rocket launcher used on air-to-ground attacks. The Royal Navy lost six Sea Harriers, two by enemy fire and four in accidents. In addition, the British lost twenty-three helicopters, nineteen of which were in accidents or sunk in vessels.

MoD ref: H3291/1

While the British advanced on Port Stanley from San Carlos, other amphibious landings were made between 6 and 8 June at Bluff Cove. Bitter fighting followed, but the Argentine forces surrendered on 14 June. Those killed in the Task Force numbered 255 servicemen and civilians, with 777 injured. Of

the injured, more than 700 were back in full employment within a few months. Argentine losses were much higher, and over 14,500 became prisoners of war before being repatriated.

MoD ref: H3282/1

The British enlarged the airfield at Port Stanley with about 7,000 feet of runway and a parallel taxiway. Arrester gear and a parking apron were also installed. Steel matting was obtained from the US Marines to help in this process. The airfield was littered with wrecked aircraft. It was estimated that the Argentine Air Force lost 117 aircraft, of which over half were helicopters. In addition, the Task Force captured about thirty other aircraft.

MoD ref: 3298/1

The RAF remained on the Falklands for defensive purposes, as demonstrated in this photograph of armed airmen filing into their Mess for a meal.

MoD ref: H3276/1

With the seasons reversed in the southern hemisphere, the RAF arrived in the Falklands at the onset of winter but only tented accommodation was available at first. The men commented that they had been told to expect a 'temperate climate'.

MoD H3298/1

The Panavia Tornado GR1, a two-seat aircraft with variable wing geometry and an unrivalled capacity for supersonic tactical strikes, earned a place in RAF history when it entered squadron service in January 1982. It was followed by the supersonic interceptor version, the Tornado F2, in April 1987. This Tornado GR1, serial ZA560 of 617 Squadron at RAF Marham in Norfolk, was photographed with Hawk T1 serial XX288 of 2 Tactical Weapons Unit at RAF Chivenor in Devon. In 1995, this Tornado was on the strength of the Tri-National Tornado Training Establishment at RAF Cottesmore in Rutland, while the Hawk was on the strength of 4 Flying Training School at RAF Valley in Anglesey.

MoD ref: PRB7107

The Lockheed TriStar K1 civil airliner entered RAF service in 1983 with 216 Squadron at Brize Norton in Oxfordshire, in order to fulfil a requirement for a long-range tanker following experience in the Falklands War. It is the heaviest aircraft in RAF service. This photograph is of serial ZD949, one of six purchased for the tanker role.

MoD ref: TN9884/3

The BAe Nimrod AEW proved a great disappointment. After many years of work and the expenditure of vast amounts of public money, the project for providing the RAF with an Airborne Early Warning aircraft built in Britain was cancelled in December 1986, in favour of the Boeing AEW Sentry. This Nimrod AEW, serial XZ285, is now stored at RAF Abingdon in Berkshire.

MoD ref: K14/4/309

When Iraqi troops invaded Kuwait in the early hours of 2 August 1990, one of the casualties was this Boeing 747 of British Airways which landed with 367 passengers en route from Heathrow to Madras and Kuala Lumpur. Some of the passengers were held as hostages and the airliner was later blown up by the Iraqis. Four days after this invasion, King Fahd of Saudi Arabia invited foreign governments to send armed forces to protect his country from Iraq. President Bush ordered US forces to prepare operation Desert Shield, in which Britain and many other countries participated under the authority of the Security Council of the United Nations. Under pressure, President Saddam Hussein of Iraq accepted on 6 December 1990 that foreign nationals could leave Kuwait and Iraq, thus abandoning his previous policy of using some of them as 'human shields' at targets which might be attacked by the Coalition Forces.

MoD ref: G92/1/1

On 8 August, the British government announced that it intended to send forces to the Gulf area. Twenty-five Hercules of the Lyneham Transport Wing were committed to the lift of equipment and personnel, with aircraft drawn from 24, 30, 47 and 70 Squadrons as well as from 242 Operational Conversion Unit. The operation began three days later, using Akrotiri in Cyprus as a staging post to and from King Khalid International Airport near Riyadh in Saudi Arabia. Some aircrews flew in excess of nineteen hours a day on this urgent task.

MoD ref: G88/24/1

Hangars at King Khalid International Airport were used to store the immense quantity of supplies brought over by the Lyneham Transport Wing and other transport aircraft. From 1 November, the RAF set up an Air Transport Detachment at this airport for internal distribution of freight and personnel.

MoD ref: G28/4/1

From the beginning of October, British troops were airlifted in the Hercules, mostly from Germany but routed through Lyneham. Puma and other helicopters were also carried. In addition to King Khalid International Airport, the Hercules flew to Dhahran in Saudi Arabia and Thumrait in Oman, with operations continuing by day and night.

MoD ref: G26/1/1

In addition to airports in the Gulf area, the Hercules flew to landing zones in the forward areas of the desert, after these had been prepared by the Royal Engineers. The sharp stones caused wear and tear to the tyres while the landing strips soon became rutted and needed repair. This Hercules

C1, serial XV192, retained its standard camouflage at the time the photograph was taken. None of these aircraft were lost in the war.

MoD ref: G86/8/1

Twelve Jaguar GR1As from 6, 41 and 54 Squadrons of the Coltishall Wing left Britain on 11 August for Thumrait in Oman, with personnel from Coltishall and 226 Operational Conversion Unit at Lossiemouth. In early October this composite squadron moved to Muharraq in Bahrain, were it was integrated into the command structure of the Coalition Air Forces. These Jaguars were replaced later in October by twelve which had been fitted up at Coltishall with more sophisticated equipment and pylons for Sidewinder air-to-air missiles. Replacement personnel also arrived during November and early December. This Jaguar, serial XZ119, of 41 Squadron was photographed while taking off from Muharraq.

MoD ref: G31/16/1

The Jaguar GR1As at Muharraq began operations in daylight on 17 January 1991, when the Desert Storm air war started. They flew initially against targets such as missile sites on the coast of Kuwait and naval vessels. From 11 February some also flew on photo-reconnaissance sorties with camera pods. When the ground war began on 24 February they attacked troop concentrations, artillery, barracks and storage areas. They carried weapons such as 1,000 lb free-fall bombs, cluster-bombs, electronic counter-measure pods, rocket-launcher pods and Sidewinder missiles. The 1,000 lb general-purpose bomb awaiting loading in this photograph is labelled 'SHARON & SOPHIE'S SADDAM SKULLCRUSHER'. The aircraft was already fitted with an overwing AIM-9L Sidewinder missile and was being loaded with a BL755 cluster-bomb. Although they completed over 600 missions and frequently came under fire, all twelve Jaguars survived the conflict.

MoD ref: G27/5/1

Tornado GR1s arrived at Muharraq in Bahrain from 29 August 1990, at Tabuk in Saudi Arabia from 8 October, and at Dhahran in Saudi Arabia from 3 January 1991. About twenty-four aircrews and other personnel were drawn from 9, 14, 15, 16, 17, 20, 27, 31 and 617 Squadrons, while aircraft were provided from RAF Brüggen and RAF Laarbruch. The GR1s commenced operations on 16/17 January, the first night of Desert Storm. Attacks on the first three nights were at low level against Iraqi airfields, employing huge JP233 dispensers being loaded as shown in this photograph. These weapons ejected runway-cratering bombs from the rear section and anti-personnel mines from the front section. After these initial attacks, the Tornados began dropping free-fall bombs from higher level on bridges and other targets. From 2 February they carried Paveway laser-guided bombs, with Buccaneers 'marking' the targets with Pavespike designator pods. On 6 February five more Tornado GR1s arrived, equipped with Thermal Imaging and Airborne Laser Designator (TIALD) pods, which enabled the bombs to be delivered with even more accuracy and without the assistance of the Buccaneers. About forty GR1s flew in the Gulf War and their rate of loss was the highest of all the Coalition Air Forces, six on operations and one in an accident.

In addition, about thirty Tornado F1s served in the conflict, arriving from 11 August 1990, with aircraft and personnel drawn from 5, 11, 23, 25, 29 and 43 Squadrons. These carried out combat air patrols and there were no losses.

Lastly, six Tornado GR1As from 2 and 13 Squadrons arrived at Dhahran on 14 January 1991, equipped with highly sophisticated reconnaissance equipment to hunt for the mobile and elusive Scud missile launchers. These also carried out excellent work and there were no losses.

MoD ref: G19/12/1

The personnel for the twelve Buccaneers were drawn from 12 and 208 Squadrons and 237 Operational Conversion Unit, forming a composite squadron. Buccaneers had served in RAF squadrons since October 1969, and in the FAA for several years beforehand. However, they were to give a remarkably good account of themselves in operations during early 1991.

MoD ref: G56/17/1

Twelve Buccaneer S2Bs from the Lossiemouth Wing flew out to Muharraq in Bahrain between 26 January and 8 February 1991, their main task being laser designation for the Tornado GR1s operating from that base and from Dhahran in Saudi Arabia. This Buccaneer was armed with a Sidewinder air-to-air missile.

MoD ref: G50/27/1

(*Opposite, bottom*) Iraq's most feared weapon was the ground-launched Scud missile, which had a 330 lb conventional warhead and a range of about 375 miles. Although inaccurate, it also had the capability of carrying a chemical or nuclear warhead. Scuds were fired from mobile launchers which were widely dispersed and could be quickly moved from one site to another, thus making their detection and destruction extremely difficult. The first were fired against Israel before dawn on 18 January 1991, causing some casualties in Haifa and Tel Aviv. They posed a serious political and psychological threat, for if Israel entered the war, the Arab countries in the Coalition might break away. The problem was resolved by deploying US Patriot anti-missile missiles in Israel, which destroyed a number of incoming Scuds and assuaged Israeli anger. Other Scuds were destroyed by British SAS mobile units operating in Iraq, calling in air strikes on occasions.

MoD ref: G91/7/1

Men of the RAF Regiment on guard around Tornado dispersals. The Regiment deployed twelve units for the operation, mainly employed on ground defence and guard duties. Its contribution was significant, for the men made up 20 per cent of the RAF's strength in the Gulf War, from a force which comprised less than 3 per cent of the RAF's manpower.

MoD ref: G37/22

The Buccaneers began operating in daylight on 2 February 1991, each carrying a Pavespike laser designator pod, a Sidewinder missile for defence and an electronic counter-measures pod. Two Buccaneers accompanied four Tornados carrying 1,000 lb Paveway laser-guided bombs, all refuelled en route by Victor K2 tankers. Near the target they split into units of two Tornados and one Buccaneer. When a Tornado released its bombs from high level, the Buccaneer designated the target with the laser and continued to track it until the impact of the bombs. From 24 February, the Buccaneers also dropped laser-guided bombs and 'self-designated' the target with their Pavespikes. None of these aircraft were lost in the conflict.

MoD ref: G54/4/1

Eight Victor K2 tankers of 55 Squadron were deployed in the Gulf War, the first flying out from RAF Marham to Muharraq in Bahrain on 14 December 1990. Their duty was air-to-air refuelling of RAF Tornados and Jaguars throughout operation Desert Storm, and they also carried out the same task with carrier-based aircraft of the US Navy.

MoD ref: G33/15/1

This airman was photographed while taking a nap on a bomb trolley bearing four Tactical Munitions Dispensers (TMDs) which were carried by USAF aircraft such as the Lockheed F-16 Fighting Falcon in the Gulf War. The weapon dispensed a mixture of anti-personnel and anti-armour mines.

MoD ref: G55/33/1

Nineteen Puma HC1s formed part of Britain's Support Helicopter Force, drawn from 230 Squadron at RAF Gütersloh and 33 Squadron at RAF Odiham. They were air-freighted from RAF Brize Norton from 1 November 1990 onwards. The Support Helicopter Force was based initially at Al Jubail in Saudi Arabia, but on 21 January 1991 it moved to Riyadh and then up to King Khalid Military City near the border with Kuwait. When the ground war began on 24 February, named operation Desert Sabre, the Pumas flew in close support of the fast-moving British Army, carrying troops and supplies while operating from improvised airstrips in Kuwait and Iraq. All the RAF's helicopters survived the conflict. This photograph is of Puma serial XW224 of 230 Squadron.

MoD ref: G82/5/1

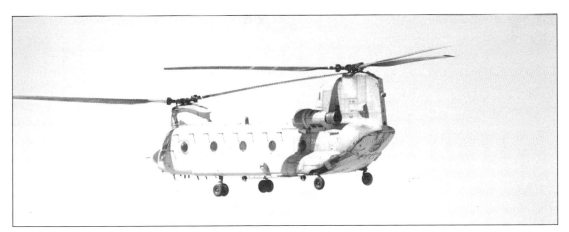

Fifteen Chinook HC1s joined Britain's Support Helicopter Force, drawn from 7 Squadron at Odiham and 18 Squadron at Gütersloh. Three were air-freighted on 24 November 1990, eight arrived by sea on 6 January 1991 and four were air-freighted in the same month. They transported troops and equipment before and during the ground war and some occasionally operated at night. Sea Kings and Lynxes of the Royal Navy formed part of the Support Helicopter Force, arriving from warships. This photograph shows Chinook serial ZA684 of the RAF's 7 Squadron.

MoD ref: G64/36/1

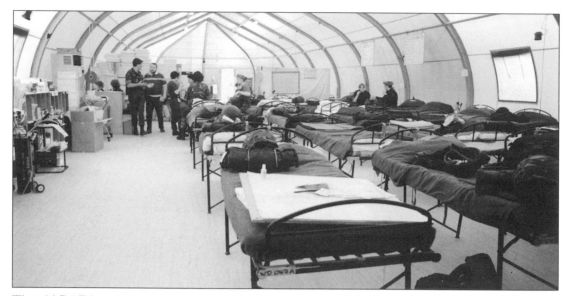

The old RAF hospital at Muharraq in Bahrain was reopened during the Gulf War and staffed with RAF doctors and orderlies, together with flight nursing officers and flight nurses of the Princess Mary's Royal Air Force Nursing Service. These essential personnel also served with mobile field hospitals and No. 1 Aeromedical Evacuation Squadron in Saudi Arabia, while similar staff stood by at RAF Akrotiri and RAF Brize Norton. Fortunately RAF casualties were not numerous.

MoD ref: G32/13/1

The Iraqi forces began to withdraw from Kuwait on 26 February 1991, using every vehicle available, but they were cut off by American and British armoured units before they could reach Basra. The road was soon littered with vehicles wrecked by shelling and air attacks.

MoD ref: G69/23/1

By 27 February, it was claimed that 3,000 of an estimated total of 4,300 Iraqi tanks had been destroyed, as well as 1,850 of 2,900 armoured personnel carriers and 2,140 of 3,100 artillery weapons. Iraqi personnel were surrendering everywhere, terrified in case they received the brutal treatment they had meted out to the Kuwaiti nationals and Coalition prisoners.

MoD ref: G59/20/1

At the end of February 1991, Iraq agreed to implement all the resolutions of the Security Council and President Bush ordered a cease-fire to take effect at 08.00 hours Baghdad time on 1 March 1991. By this time, it was estimated that 100,000 Iraqis had been killed with the same number captured, in contrast to less than 500 killed among the Coalition forces. Fortunately for the Iraqi prisoners, they received humane treatment from the front-line forces, being given medical attention as well as food and water.

MoD ref: G85/35/1

TOWARDS THE MILLENNIUM

The Hawker Siddeley Buccaneer entered RAF squadron service in October 1969, several years after it had been introduced into the Fleet Air Arm. A two-seater with a speed of Mach 0.92 at sea level, it fulfilled the role of a low-level strike and reconnaissance aircraft. However, it was also found suitable for low-level penetration work in RAF Germany. During the Gulf War, Buccaneers with laser designator pods directed bombs dropped by Tornados onto their targets. The highly successful Buccaneer remained in service with Strike Command until 1994. This photograph of Buccaneers of 208 Squadron flying over the Severn Bridge was taken on 21 July 1975. Squadron Leader Peter Jones (OC B Flight) and Flight Lieutenant Peter Hill were in one aircraft, with Flight Lieutenant Dave Symonds and Squadron Leader Graham Pitchfork (OC A Flight) in the other.

MoD ref: TN7326/29

When it was supplied to the RAF's 1 Squadron in July 1969, the remarkable British Aerospace Harrier GR1 became the first 'vertical take-off and landing' aircraft to enter squadron service with any air force. It is a single-seater capable of a maximum speed of Mach 0.95, employed mainly for ground attack, as was demonstrated during the Falklands War. This Harrier, serial XV279, was one of the development aircraft, photographed at RAF Upavon in Wiltshire on 24 May 1967. In 1995, this machine was used for Weapons Loading Training at RAF Wittering in Northamptonshire.

MoD ref: PRB36900

The Westland/Aérospatiale Puma HC1 entered RAF squadron service in June 1971, replacing the Whirlwind helicopter for ground assault and troop transport. Pumas have served in Germany, Belize, Cyprus, Northern Ireland and the Arabian Gulf. Several of these helicopters remained operational in 1995. This photograph of the Pumas of 230 Operational Conversion Unit at Odiham in Hampshire was taken when flying over the Needles off the Isle of Wight.

MoD ref: TN6368/35

The Sepecat Jaguar GR1 single-seat fighter first entered RAF operational service in March 1974. Eight squadrons in Germany were eventually equipped with Jaguars, which can achieve Mach 1.6 and also carry out the role of ground attack. Jaguar GR1, serial XZ374 (in the foreground) of 20 Squadron at Brüggen in Germany was photographed with a Harrier GR3 when the squadron converted to Jaguars in 1977. In 1995, this machine was still in service with the School of Technical Training at RAF Cosford in Shropshire. Jaguar GR1As, the reconnaissance version, remain in service at RAF Coltishall in Norfolk.

MoD ref: 1830–1

The Boeing Vertol Chinook, with twin rotors, entered RAF squadron service in August 1981. It is a medium-lift helicopter with a crew of four and the capacity for transporting thirty troops or up to 28,000 lb of freight. This Chinook of 18 Squadron was photographed when based at Gütersloh in Germany. The detachment moved there from Odiham in Hampshire in August 1983, after a detachment had served in the Falklands War.

MoD ref: RAFG/107/83/PR

The British Aerospace Hawk T1 is an advanced jet trainer which first entered RAF service in November 1976. As with the Shorts Tucano, the two seats of this aircraft are arranged in tandem. This Hawk TIA, serial XX258, was photographed while carrying a Sea Eagle, an air-to-surface missile with a range of about 60 miles made by British Aerospace Dynamics. In 1995 the aircraft was on the strength of the Central Flying School at RAF Valley in Anglesey.

MoD ref: C3172/B

The Boeing AEW Sentry began operational service with 8 Squadron at RAF Waddington in Lincolnshire during 1991, after a working-up and training period. Adapted from the Boeing 707 airliner and fitted with an enormous rotodome radar antenna for airborne early warning, this aircraft had already seen many years of service with the USAF and NATO. The squadron is equipped with seven Sentries, such as serial ZA104 in this photograph taken by Sergeant Rick Brewell. This aircraft commemorates 80 years of the squadron's continuous service in the RFC and RAF from 1 January 1915.

MoD ref: 836/12

The McDonnell Douglas Phantom was ordered from the USA to fill a gap in RAF requirements, the FG1 as an interceptor and the FG2 for ground attack and reconnaissance. It was a two-seater with a maximum speed of Mach 2.1 and the first machines entered operational service in May 1969. The F3 interceptor, with an improved performance and more sophisticated weapons system, equipped 74 Squadron from March 1984. This Phantom F3, with 56 Squadron markings on the

front and 74 Squadron markings on the tail, was the final year display machine. Flown by Squadron Leader Archie Liggatt with Flight Lieutenant Mark Mainwaring as navigator, it was photographed over the north coast of Norfolk on 8 July 1992 by Sergeant Rick Brewell.

MoD ref: 694/7

A Tornado GR1A of 13 Squadron from Marham in Norfolk, photographed by Sergeant Rick Brewell while flying over Scarborough in Yorkshire. At the same base 2 Squadron is also equipped with this highly sophisticated aircraft, employed on tactical reconnaissance.

MoD ref: 623/95

The EH101 multi-role helicopter is produced by EH Industries, formed by the companies Westland and Augusta. This photograph taken by Petty Officer Fez Parker is of the Royal Navy variant, named the Merlin. A variant is under order for the RAF but has not yet been delivered.

MoD ref: 95/132/6

INDEX